Modern Slavery

Modern Slavery

The Story of My American Dream

Ernestine D. Motouom

ISBN: 978-0-578-45305-7

This book does not depict any relational issues between black and white in the workplace.

To my mother, Anne Marie, with love,
for denying herself and sacrificing her life for the sake
of her children

Contents

Epilogue

This book comes from my personal experiences in the workplace and also from narratives I got from people I encountered in my journey at work. It explores the difficulties and problems employees encounter at work under heartless managers who put them on hectic schedules and care little about their physical ability to handle work under prolonged schedules and mandatory overtime. This reality is consistent with the claim that a slavery mentality still hovers over American society. In the traditional slavery system, slaves had food as a sole reward. Likewise, today's low income is just enough to put food on the table. With such slave-like incomes, workers can neither file for a retirement plan nor muster the financial ability to send their kids to college. In addition, they cannot afford health insurance and cannot buy houses. Some may obtain low-priced insurance coverage, but it comes with a high deductible that protects insurers from paying hospital bills, unless the patient pays in full the assigned deductible.

I have come to notice firsthand that, due to the unfriendly and tedious work environment, workers do not have any choice but to use stimulants in order to deal with the discomfort and pain that come with prolonged schedules and mandatory overtime. Some employers put pain pills at their employees' disposal, or they bring their own. They use energy drinks, ibuprofen, pain patches, and knee braces as survival tools to manage their pain. They look fit in their outer appearance, but the body is eventually and gradually broken down. When their health is damaged as a result of work-related stress and the abuse of stimulants, the health-care system denies them adequate service. It has been proven that low-income people have problems accessing health services due to elevated cost.

The health-care billing system in the United States is a scam. I have used my personal experience from abroad to prove that elevated hospital costs in this country stem solely from greed and are not correlated with the quality of services rendered.

The capitalist system puts a strain on the emancipation of the poor. They find themselves trapped, suffocated, and molded in poverty. The freedom that comes with capitalism gives businesspeople the right to deny the poor a decent income for their hard work while they live in opulent extravagance, spending their overflow on lavish lifestyles and futile pleasures. I used to think that in a developed country like this, education was a great path out of poverty. Unfortunately, it is not true. The establishment of for-profit schools and universities constitutes a trap and stumbling block for US citizens and especially individuals from poor backgrounds. These schools within the US system offer affordable programs that attract poor folks. However, most of their programs are unaccredited. As a consequence, students who enroll in such programs are less likely to get a job, finding themselves buried in debt that they may never be able to pay off.

Introduction

History recounts that people were forced to perform hard tasks during slavery with food as their only payment. Slave owners heartlessly used whips and other forms of torture as their preferred disciplinary methods. Slaves carried out endless hours of work, whether under the scorching sun or in rainy conditions. For ages, parents and their offspring labored hopelessly in sorrow for the well-being of their masters. History reveals that the Israelites were oppressed in slavery for more than four hundred years, while the oppression of Africans lasted three hundred years. In such an unfortunate situation, slaves most likely felt that the slimy pit was their destination, with no hope of escape. The Bible states that the Israelites cried out to God, and he answered their prayers, sending Moses the Liberator. In the

United States, antislavery movements advocated for abolition, which resulted in the Thirteenth Amendment. Unlike the Israelites who left the country of their masters for the Promised Land, Africans in the United States did not have any option other than to mingle with those who once owned them. For both blacks and ex-slave owners, a brand new life began. On the one hand, blacks were celebrating freedom, while on the other hand, ex-slave masters were devastated by the loss of free labor and its negative impact on their economic landscape. Freedom came with new challenges, among which was the issue of unemployment coupled with all sorts of discriminations. Once freed, blacks quickly found themselves in desperate situations. Some had to go back to their former masters begging for paid work. Others migrated to pursue a better life. Some did find jobs, from both ex-slave owners and those who had never owned slaves. Unfortunately, none received decent treatment. Freedom was granted, but the freed remained at the mercy of the dominant white population. Blacks had freedom but could not control their fate. They still leaned on white folks for daily bread, still a slavery-like remuneration that was barely enough to fill their stomachs. Of course, no one believes that the day after slave abolition and the emancipation of blacks, lives would suddenly have improved. However, a reasonable expectation would be to see things change with time. Obviously, right after the abolition of slavery, the very masters who mistreated, tortured, and murdered slaves would not suddenly treat them with dignity and respect, consider them to be equal, and change overnight from oppressors to friends. Yet, one would expect such changes eventually to occur.

Indeed, changes have taken place over time, but inequality between blacks and whites remains rampant in the United States. One such area is income inequality. During slavery, Africans gathered crumbs under their masters' tables to feed themselves. Despite the current economic boom, this has not changed. The vast majority of African Americans struggle in poverty. The only difference now is that they are not the only group of people gathering crumbs under rich people's tables. The misery club now includes a percentage of white, Latinos, and other ethnic groups. The misery of the black population during slavery was orchestrated and fashioned by a class of people who viewed themselves as superior; likewise, poverty in the United States of our day is fashioned and molded by rich folks. Without exaggeration, a slavery mentality is still hovering over America in the twenty-first century. The minimum wage and harsh working conditions in most American industries speak for that. If not, could one explain why CEOs and executive board members of companies earn multimillion-dollar salaries coupled with huge bonuses, while someone in the production chain earns just above seven dollars an hour as gross income? Although the United States is considered first among all developed countries, the superpower also has one of the lowest minimum wages. If you are asking yourself why, greed might be at the root of the problem. In US history, people have fought for all kinds of rights, such as the right to sit in the front of public transportation and the right to vote, but the fight for adequate rewarding of hard work or a decent income has been left in the hands of politicians. Recently, President Obama and his administration attempted without success to raise the minimum hourly wage from $7.25 to $10.10. In reality, even this would have been insufficient to get most workers out of poverty due to the high cost of living in the United States. The poverty issue in the United States is not limited to the income level, but involves poor working conditions and hectic work schedules that push people to indulge in risky behaviors, jeopardizing their health.

Chapter 1

Hectic Work Schedules and Poor Working Conditions

Ever since I arrived in the United States in 2006, I have asked myself why cashiers in various retail stores are not given the chance to sit while serving customers, as they are in Europe, where we lived before moving here. The only universal answer seems to be "high productivity." Even though I have never worked in such conditions, my concern is that it would be very hard and tedious for someone to be on his/her feet all shift long. Thumbs up to companies like Aldi, J. P. Morgan Warehouse, and others for providing better working conditions for employees, who I am sure are very grateful. The question I ask myself is whether cashiers in stores requiring the standing position perform faster and better than those in Aldi. I am not sure about that. My personal speculation is that cashiers who are forced to be on their feet all shift long become tired faster than those who relax in the sitting position while serving customers and get up to tackle other tasks when the customer line is empty. I know from personal experience that a worn-out body naturally slows down. Cashiers in industries that require them to stand all shift long could end the shift with back pain and sore feet, while Aldi's cashiers, for example, are less likely to suffer such pain, at least in the short term. Should I mention that Aldi is a store of German origin that treats its employees with decency and dignity?

The same wheel of torture has been set up in many warehouses. Moved by the spirit of high productivity, most warehouse jobs are designed for employees to stand on their feet for ten to twelve hours and more. If companies are not willing to design sittable work stations or allow some tasks to be done in a sitting position, why not, at least for the sake of human well-being, shorten the shift length and hire more people? This would boost the economy by cutting down the unemployment rate and reducing the number of individuals on welfare or safety net programs.

Once, a recruiting agent hired me and sent me to a warehouse, warning me how hard the work would be.

"Believe me, I worked there before, and it is hard," she said. "You will be on your feet all day long, and this comes with a lot of pain."

Not fully understanding what she was alluding to, I thought she just wanted to scare me away.

"In what department do you prefer to work?" she went ahead and asked.

At that time I remembered watching a video at home depicting the various departments and the tasks performed there but wasn't sure which one would suit me best. Given the fear that seized me after hearing her talk about the task challenges, I opted to let her decide my fate.

"I do not know," I replied.

After explaining what tasks were performed in each department, she expected me to make up my own mind after all. Unfortunately, I was already scared and afraid I would pick the most difficult task and regret it afterward.

"I am still not sure," I told her.

"OK! I am going to put you in the return department," she said.

"OK!" I replied.

"You will be in one spot on your feet all day long," she added.

"OK!" I replied.

Had she selected the best position for me? I mean, was it the least stressful? I asked myself but couldn't provide an answer. The alternatives were to walk ten to fifteen miles on a flat floor or climb up and down the stairs all shift long.

On the day of orientation, we were told the same thing regarding the harshness of tasks. She told us that during her first weeks of work, the pain in her back and feet was nearly unbearable.

"I had to find some hot pads for pain relief after every shift," she told us. She added that the company had some pain pills at our disposal for free, in case of need. "You will definitely need them," she stated. She wasn't trying to scare us away, even though it sounded very scary, but rather to provide us with needed survival tools.

My first day of work was coming up the following week. From what I had heard from the staffing agency and during orientation, I knew I would be on my feet all shift long (ten hours), as would the other associates. However, I did not expect to see recruiting staffing representatives and shift leaders on their feet too. These were people in charge of supervision and paperwork. Their tables were elevated with their computers placed at a corner or in the center of the table. A medium-sized man would have the table at his chest, too high to lean on when you feel tired. I did not comprehend why these leaders were denied comfortable seats. My speculation regarding such working conditions is this: "Before you get the mighty dollar, you must strive and endure pain for it." Slaves had to suffer just for food, and that mentality is still hovering in some US industries today.

In my second week of work there, my back was already in so much pain and my feet so sore that I could barely walk. They noticed quickly that I was in trouble because from time to time, I stretched in order to keep going. It wasn't that I was lifting heavy items; nothing that I processed was actually above my ability to handle, being just clothes, shoes, and other light items. They rushed to make me sign a slip of paper testifying that they taught me all appropriate methods of transferring and lifting, in order to protect the company from a potential Lawsuit, I guess. I remembered that free pain pills were available to us. However, I did not want to go down that dangerous path. Pills give people under those conditions a false sense of "everything is OK," while the body is, in reality, breaking down.

Changing working conditions and/or shortening the shift are appropriate solutions to the pain problem. We had three breaks of fifteen minutes per shift. Even though this was very helpful, I found those fifteen minutes to be too short. Depending on the location of the assigned workstation, one could walk two to three minutes to reach the break room, meaning that the actual break could be somewhere between nine and eleven minutes. The worst case was when one needed a detour to the restroom; the entire break time could even be used up because of the line formed by restroom users. To fully enjoy my break, I decided to use the restroom afterward and wasn't the only one thinking that way; indeed, whether one went to the restroom during or after break, the line was inevitable. This became an issue that the manager quickly addressed. We were said to be sitting on the clock, hindering productivity. After every lunch break, he gave a summary of our productivity as well as the total amount of time lost. He called upon everyone to return to their respective workstations as quickly as possible to avoid time loss. In order to reinforce that, the supervisors started writing down the names of those who delayed in getting back to work after breaks. I was one of them. Under such pressure, I started to avoid using the restroom during my break, even though I knew it wasn't good for my health. I was, and others who did the same were, running the risk of bladder enlargement in the long run. But who cares? High productivity is name of the game.

Work schedules at Warehouse I were better than those I found at Warehouse II. Even though a shift was ten hours, the supervisors at Warehouse I made sure every employee had at least two days off every week, and sometimes three, if we were not called for mandatory overtime. Thumbs-up for that. These days off were very helpful; however, I was in continuous pain from prolonged muscle strain, and any home duties requiring standing, like cooking or mowing, aggravated the pain.

After two weeks of work at Warehouse I, I had minor outpatient surgery. I was told by the staffing agent that the company did not accept any excuse notes from any doctor, which sounded very weird and depicted discrimination against people with health conditions. By the time I had the job interview, my surgery was already scheduled. At that time, I wished the surgery had already been performed or that I had applied for the position only after the surgery. However, it was too late. Their implemented point system would kick me out after the surgery. Thank God, I had a glimpse of hope. My doctor told me that some people go back to work right after that surgery. Unfortunately, my case did not turn out that way. Under the effects of narcotic pills, I could not help but stay in bed for more than a week. I had never been exposed to such drugs before. It was then that I learned that some people are addicted to those pills. I still don't understand the rationale behind those addictions. "How could someone get there?" I asked myself. Those pills made me feel dizzy and weary.

I did not intend to quit my job because of sickness. When the surgery date was approaching, I brought my case to the staffing representative, who reiterated that they did not accept any excuse notes from doctors.

"Why should I lose my job? Why shouldn't I be given a chance to come back? I did not choose to get sick," I told him. "Why? Why? Why?"

After pressuring him with many questions, he gave me a glimpse of hope. "As long as you call in every single day you are out of work, you might have a chance to come back, but there is no guarantee," he told me. He added that for each day off, one must call in and make sure to save the confirmation number for each call, which I did. At least it was something to lean on.

After my stitches were taken out, my dizziness kept bothering me. However, I was determined to resume work if I was given another chance. To my surprise, the recruiting agent did not even look at the note I brought from the doctor's office, saying that she was sorry, but they did not take doctors' notes. After I insisted, she finally gave up and sent the company an email, telling me that they may or may not call me back. She couldn't give me any guarantee. I walked out of her office with a dejected spirit. At least I tried, I told myself. On my way home, I felt dizzy while driving, a sign to me that it wasn't worth taking any risk. Whether they called me or not, that chapter of my life was closed. They did, in fact, call and invite me to come to work the next day, stating that I should come in a little bit early to get a new badge, but it was too late; I had already made up my mind. Their initial resistance just shocked me. Even though I called in each day as requested and provided confirmation numbers, my badge had been deactivated. I was already tagged as fired, resigned, retired, or the like.

Warehouse II had the most chaotic work schedules. It belonged to a very successful cell phone industry with a branch in Louisville, Kentucky. Due to business growth, a second building was constructed to handle the large number of orders they received. I was assigned a position in the second building. If it had not been for their hectic schedules and poor management, it would have been a beautiful place to work. Many colleagues I spoke to wanted to make a career there, but these problems drove them away. After searching for a position in my field of expertise (public health) for two years without success, I lost all hope; I decided to make a career with the cell phone industry at Warehouse II, if possible. But that dream was also shattered.

It was amazing that Warehouse II was just eight minutes away from home. What a privilege! Some workers drove nearly two hours to get to work. Because I was prepared by my previous experience in Warehouse I, I had no apprehension or fear of the unknown. After standing on my feet all day long, what else could happen? Back pain, sore feet…oh yes! Do I have a choice? Like many other workers, I had needs to fulfill.

It did not take long for me to realize how chaotic their management system was. The abuse of power from the manager was outrageous. The staffing agency told me that the first shift I applied for was from 7:00 a.m. to 3:30 p.m. After orientation, we were asked without further explanation to come in at 5:00 a.m. on our first day of work. I did not understand the discrepancy regarding the starting time but did not really care much. After all, I had a job after a long time of unemployment.

We were about twelve employees on our first day of work at Warehouse II, recruited as temp-to-hire employees. We were very fortunate that our various staffing representatives showed up on time. The group that started the following week had to sit in the break room for two hours before their representatives walked in at 7:00 a.m. with their badges. Why were these people treated like that? I asked myself. Couldn't the warehouse staff and the recruiting agency communicate to get things done appropriately? It was later that I learned that the decision to bring people in at 5:00 a.m. or 7:00 a.m. mostly depended on the manager's mood. Staffing agents probably were lost or confused in that game. The other employees and I were confused as well. After requiring us to come in three days in a row at 5:00 a.m. during our first week of work, I thought they might have changed the starting time. Around 1:30 p.m., we ran out of work. Only four of us showed up on the fourth day. We did not really wonder about this, thinking that the other colleagues just happened to be late. After clocking in, a Warehouse II employee came to us and asked us to clock out.

"Why?" we asked him.

"Because your shift starts at 7:00 a.m. today," he replied, adding, "I am sorry. You'll have to wait in the break room till 7:00 a.m. before you can clock in."

"What is going on?" we asked.

"The shift leader asked everybody yesterday to come in today at 7:00 a.m.," he replied.

"He did not accurately convey that message, and that's why we are here," we told him.

"The shift leader asked me to pass the message down to you. You'll have to wait in the break room till he gets here," he said.

"Do you know at what time we get up to be here now, sir?" one of us asked him.

"Sorry, but you must clock out," he replied.

After resisting the ugly request of clocking out, the shift leader gave him phone instructions to keep us busy until he arrived. In fact, after we ran out of work on the day before, we were dispatched on the floor for house-keeping, as it was routinely done; the shift leader passed down the critical information to some but did not ensure that everybody had it. Yet he expected to use his power as shift leader to abuse us. We resisted that day, but I fell into a trap the following day. I had to leave early for an appointment and forgot to ask what time the shift would start the next day. It was too late to call when it came to my mind, and it was difficult to decide whether to get there at 5:00 a.m. or 7:00 a.m. the next day. As usual in such situations, I selected the wrong option. Given the ongoing point system, I would bank some points if I arrived at 7:00 a.m. for a shift starting at 5:00 a.m. I had already banked one point for leaving early the day before and did not want to collect more. So arriving at 5:00 a.m. seemed to be a smart decision, even though I risked sitting in the break room for two unproductive hours. That is exactly what happened. To my surprise, I was not the only one in this situation. A male employee also arrived early and claimed nobody informed him. I wasn't surprised at all, since he had selected housekeeping as his main task, and was traveling the whole floor all shift long. Still, it was the responsibility of the manager or shift leader to make sure everyone was informed. Apparently, they did not care. Their decision about the time to begin the shift was not always based on the volume of orders received. On many occasions, after having having very unproductive hours due to lack of work, we would reclock into the spe-cial hours label and wander around doing housekeeping or anything outside of our main task before being sent home early with the request to show up the next day at 5:00 a.m. And the cycle continued.

Warehouse II had two separated buildings. I was selected to work in Building 2, which was smaller than Building 1. About eight to ten tables were lined up in the center of the building. On our first day of work, the shift leader asked us to sit two by two at each table. A few minutes later, he brought us pallets loaded with containers of phones; he assigned one pallet per table plus an empty pallet to each table on which the processed container would be placed. Each container had five retail T-Mobile boxes with one cell phone inside. He brought two stacks of different stickers as well. One sticker carried new ad information, and the other had information about new product features.

After gathering us around one of the tables, he picked a container, and after opening it, he took out one retail box and opened it. He peeled one of the first stickers and pasted it inside the cover of the retail box; then, he pasted the other sticker on the back of the retail box. Next, he instructed us to do the same and arrogantly walked away with no further details. From that time on, any further instruction came only after mistakes occurred.

Two experienced individuals arrived later that day. One joined me at my table, and her friend or companion joined a lady at the table behind me. The one working with me quickly noticed that I did not understand an inch of the task. She looked over my shoulder, called to her friend or companion, and told her that we were not paying attention to the N-box.

What does N-box mean? I asked myself. However, I kept working with my head down. Although I listened to her complaints, I did not at any time look at her, acting just like a shy baby. The other associates did not react to her complaints either. I am sure nobody understood what she was talking about, since Latinos constituted the vast majority of that crowd, and most were not fluent in English.

The N-box was the box that carried the identification code for the whole pallet and was supposed to be placed at the right corner of the pallet on the first row.

The woman working with me went on telling her friend that we were placing processed containers randomly on the pallet. I did not budge on any of her complaints, even though she seemed right to me. Our mess and lack of knowledge irritated her so badly. You could tell that she was one of the rare employees who loves to work and does it well and with great heart. She told her friend that she could not correct our mistakes because she did not want to be bossy, since she really had no power over us. Actually, her friend did not care and was less concerned about all of that. Then she called to the shift leader as he was passing by and explained that we were placing processed containers randomly on the pallet without giving the N-box its right spot.

"Nobody showed them what to do," she told him.

"You show them!" he answered and arrogantly walked away.

"Did you hear him?" she asked her friend.

"What power do I have over these people?" she continued, before adding, "This guy is crazy and doesn't take his work seriously."

The two friends continued gossiping about things the shift leader had done wrong during past weeks. Since she was late that morning, she probably did not know that he was the one who trained us on the new assignment. Some minutes passed by, and the shift leader did not come back, so she understood that he really meant it when he asked her to train us. She went from table to table showing people how to do it correctly, except for me. My attitude might have scared her away. During the course of her debate, I did not at any time dare to look at her; I just looked down and did what I was told to do. I did not expect her to step up and take the lead. However, I was prepared to undo or redo my work anytime.

These were just a couple of mistakes she noticed at that time, and more were still to come. What I did not comprehend is that, despite suboptimal training, they expected an outstanding performance from us. Unfortunately, our first week's performance was quickly hindered by various kinds of errors, from attaching the wrong sticker on phones and mixing up pallets to placing phones in the wrong containers. As a result, a colleague was unjustly fired for faults committed because of ignorance. Normally, the shift leader or manager would have shown him mercy and saved his job, for they had failed to provide him with the appropriate training. It was very unfortunate and unfair for him to lose his job like that. This was a dedicated and hardworking Latino man who was trying to make a living. I felt deeply sorry for what happened to him. This company was the perfect place for him to work, given his language barrier. Unlike other companies where you need to master the English language to some extent, Warehouse II had designed a way to accommodate foreigners from different backgrounds. I was amazed the day we were sent to Building 1. The facility manager promptly asked what my first language was.

"French," I told her.

"OK! I will find you someone who speaks French," she replied.

"Thanks, but I am very fluent in English. I am fine with an English-speaking trainer," I replied.

It was amazing that people did not have to speak English to work in that company. The two shift leaders we had were Hispanic but also spoke English. Therefore, Hispanic associates had no integration issue.

That day he was determined to work more than anyone else, to be the first to finish processing his pallet. He did not have a table mate that day but still wanted to prove that he was the best. To this end, he needed to work at least twice as fast as any of us. From time to time, the shift leader required us to write down the time used to process a whole pallet. As we were temp-to-hire employees, I personally thought the race aimed to select the best and gave my best in order to keep the job. I believe this man eventually thought the same. He found a seemingly smart way to speed up the work: unload many containers, pour the contents on the table, and paste stickers as quickly as he could. It did work well. Although he was singly handling a whole pallet, he was well ahead of the rest of us. I remember looking at him with awe for such effort. I thought of following his example, but something within me said no. During the race, the shift leader and the manager walked in from time to time, but that particular table loaded with many phones did not catch their attention. The swift man was about to cross the finish line when the manager arrived.

"Why are there so many phones on the table?" she asked him in English.

Unfortunately, he could not understand her. He needed a translator. The manager then summoned the shift leader for translation.

Don't you see that he's pasting stickers on the containers? I asked myself.

"You should not open more than one box at a time," she said. "Each phone has to go back in its original box. How far have you gone with this?"

It was too late. He was nearly done.

It was going to take us hours to get this fixed.

As they were talking, the other associates stopped working, with every eye fixed on them, because we did not understand what the man had done wrong. He was then brought to the general manager, who fired him. That chapter of his life was over. Later on, we were summoned for a meeting that should have taken place a long time ago.

After three weeks in Warehouse II, we were moved to a different department in Building 2: the direct customer service department (D2C). Unlike other departments, we received proper training. I wished the associates had been given incentives for training new employees. Unfortunately, it was not the case. My two first weeks in the new department were very good because we maintained an eight-hour shift starting at 7:00 a.m. with Saturdays and Sundays off.

As mentioned above, the normal shift in Warehouse II was from 7:00 a.m. to 3:30 p.m.; however, supervisors might request that employees arrive as early as 5:00 a.m. if needed. This was supposed to be implemented primarily during peak season, which falls between Thanksgiving and Christmas. By the time I was hired toward the end of August, peak season was just around the corner. Thank God, I still had time to enjoy the normal schedule and at the same time worry whether I would be able to handle the peak season challenges described by senior colleagues. They said even Saturdays and Sundays would be busy. I tried to anticipate a solution for that before getting hit. As a Christian, I wanted at least Sundays to be free in order to attend church services. Why not? After working from Monday through Friday and even some Saturdays, why shouldn't I express my right to worship God on Sundays?

I went to the staffing agency and addressed my concerns. Unfortunately, I received no hope from the representative. Meanwhile, there was some tiny hope that he hid from me. Indeed, there was an option of requesting Sundays off by providing logical reasons to support the request. However, I found out about this only after my resignation. After talking to the staffing representative, he relayed my point to the manager, and this stirred up in her such animosity that it prompted my resignation, which occurred a couple of weeks later.

I could be simply paranoid or presume that gossip sparked that fire. It could have been something else. Why not? In fact, some senior colleagues considered her to be bipolar, manipulative, and verbally aggressive, with an abuse of power, which I agreed with. We heard that the company couldn't do anything about it because she would file a lawsuit if she were fired. Many people had complained about her repulsive attitude, but nothing was ever done about it and most likely would not be done. Nobody provided me with details of what went wrong between her and the company. Maybe they didn't know either, or did not want to get into the gossip game. That day, without any logical motivation, she suddenly put us on ten- to eleven-hour shifts starting at 5:00 a.m. Ten-hour shifts were normally reserved for the high demand season, but this wasn't the case. Indeed, there was no high demand, and shifts started at 5:00 a.m. working on special hours doing housekeeping tasks/cleaning because no order was in yet. This lasted for about a month, of which we worked one Sunday. During such useless overtimes, we spent about 40 to 60 percent of the time on special hours finding something, anything, to do in order to avoid sitting on the clock.

In one particular week, she sent us home early on Thursday and Friday because there was literally no work but made working that weekend mandatory. Due to family responsibility, I called in on Saturday, and the point system was used to whip me severely. I was given two points for not showing up that Saturday. Prior to that, I had banked two points due to appointments. Because of the point system, my journey, and that of many other employees there, was quickly coming to an end. Our manager in Building 2 surely had a lot of experience but lacked even basic management skills. Another whip she utilized to discipline us was the so-called write-up with no prior warning. Given that she failed to tell us the dos and don'ts on our first day of work, we learned from mistake to mistake, which came with consequences. One colleague lost his job in the first week of work; for others, getting written up was the element of correction and discipline used for first-time mistakes, with no prior verbal warning.

By the time the peak season kicked in, we were already weary of needless overtime, and I was not really ready for the additional stress associated with elevated workloads and mandatory work on Sundays.

Prior to that crisis, the eight-hour shift suited me well. At the end of the shift, I was tired but not worn out and could well enjoy my time after work, helping kids with homework and other family responsibilities. Moreover, I used weekends off to cook and freeze meals to make my weekdays easy and more enjoyable. Unfortunately, in my third week in the D2C department, schedules quickly geared up from eight hours to eleven, even on Saturdays, leaving us with only Sundays for rest. Before I knew it, I quickly ran out of frozen meals; worse, by the end of the fourth week, I had neither time nor strength to cook more. I felt indignant, mostly because it wasn't worth having us there at 5:00 a.m. and keeping us till 4:30 p.m., given the workload. As mentioned above, we started our shift on special hours/housekeeping literally with no work at all or with very little orders available. In those lean days, the Latino manager hid some stickers under her table for Hispanic associates only, and whenever a handful of orders were available, she would call them in Spanish. We would just watch them walking back with stickers in their hands.

What amazed me at that place was how much the associates loved the job. Even though we were forbidden to take more than one stack of stickers, people still did (out of the managers' sight, of course), especially during lean times with few orders. In my fourth week, even though we had an eleven-hour shift, work was readily available when we arrived in the morning and remained on the table for the second shift after us, which wasn't the case in the previous weeks. I felt compelled to climb the ladder and talk to the general manager. I was simply trying to plead for an eight-hour shift during lean times. After making it clear that I did not mind coming in early on busy days, I explained to him that we were being forced to do needless mandatory overtime. I stressed that we needed some rest, adding that employees also have family responsibilities. To my total surprise, he refused to address that issue.

"I understand that you have family responsibility," he answered me, before adding, "but here we are not flexible at all. You can resign and find something else." Further, he explained to me that sometimes T-Mobile calls them when they have something like twenty thousand orders or more, asking them to bring people in some Saturdays.

"That is exactly what I am talking about," I replied. If the manager is alerted about a large order, she could then give us a break during low demand when there are no alerts at all.

Why do we have to arrive at 5:00 a.m., labor for eleven hours, and leave second-shift employees with no work at all? The work could be evenly distributed and of no burden for either shift. I remember a second-shift worker on one of the nonbusy days pleading for me to give her my leftover stickers before leaving. There was no work available for them. Unlike nursing homes, where I have seen caregivers hide for an hour or even more, associates in that company loved their work.

After failing to find a solution to that issue, I thought I was probably the only one having trouble with such a schedule. After all, people were paid 1.5 times their hourly rates for working extra hours. I started asking questions and listening to gossip in order to have an in-depth understanding of how my colleagues perceived the situation. I quickly realized that people were angry, bitter, disgruntled, and stressed out about the situation in which they found themselves. The general feeling was that all were hanging on just to pay their bills.

"I don't know why they force us to do this many hours. Taxes will cut everything," a colleague said.

"They took four hundred on my last paycheck," said another.

"They took three hundred on mine," still another replied.

Another day in the clocking station, a colleague greeted her friend, saying, "Good morning."

The latter replied, "I don't know why I am here. I do not want to be here; too much overtime."

A colleague also told me that, in order to arrive at 5:00 a.m., she must get up at 3:00 a.m. because she lives an hour away. This was one of those days with no work available as we arrived at 5:00 a.m. Why did the supervisor treat her employees like that?

However, another colleague felt very comfortable with that situation. She explained that at her former place of work, they were forced to work ten hours every shift from Monday through Saturday. She added that at some point, people became tired of it and started not showing up on Saturdays. To reinforce the rule, the manager heartlessly started writing people up.

There is a saying that if you find yourself in an uncomfortable situation and meet someone whose case is even worse, it can give you some comfort. One of the ladies told me that they must arrive at 4:00 a.m. to sort stickers and display them on the tables so that work would be ready for us at 5:00 a.m. She added in a desperate tone, "It is too much overtime, and you don't sleep. I have to get up at 2:00 a.m. to be here at 4:00 a.m.!"

Among us was a young, hardworking Hispanic lady, the mother of a five-month-old baby. The baby would not allow her to sleep at night; as a consequence, she took pain pills as needed, to keep going at work. But how long was she taking them? She was not the only one using pain pills. This caught my attention when I saw her borrowing some from her friend.

"Are you sick?" I naively asked her.

"Oh, no" she replied, before adding, "I can't rest even at home, for I have a five-month-old baby. I am in too much pain."

Workers came in with pain pills in the clear bags allowed by the company, when they chose to do so. I did not experience this in Warehouse I. No wonder that most employees, despite their hectic schedules, looked fit and strong in outer appearance. At one point I was so exhausted that I had trouble lifting my feet. A colleague advised me to take ibuprofen. She was ready to give me some pills.

"It relaxes your muscles," she told me.

"No," I replied.

A pregnant lady also asked me to get some "energy shot" for myself.

"What it is?" I asked her.

"You don't know energy shot?" she asked in reply. "It is very helpful, boosts your strength right away and healthy. You can find it at any gas station."

Her advice really scared me at first because when I heard the word "shot," I thought it was some kind of drug injection. I was concerned that she might be on drugs despite her pregnancy and prayed for the well-being of that innocent unborn child. I declined the suggestion and expressed my concern about its effects on health. None of the above propositions sounded healthy to me. Later on I realized that energy shot referred to the well-known five-hour energy drink. What confusion! Still, energy drinks are not appropriate for pregnant women. Such energy stimulants nearly jeopardized my health years ago. Did she have a choice? She thought that it was healthy. She was working hard to prepare for the coming of her baby and unfortunately found herself in a system where the mighty dollar seems to matter more than human beings. I will elaborate more on energy drinks and their associated risk factors in chapter 3.

On the Friday of my eighth week in the D2C department, around 11:00 a.m., a Hispanic colleague whose workstation was behind mine stomped her feet on the floor repeatedly while shouting "Yes! Yes! Yes!"

"What up? What up?" I asked her.

"Tomorrow, no work," she replied.

Indeed, the Hispanic manager had just told them in Spanish that we would have that Saturday off. Only God can testify to what joy invaded our souls at the time. Finally, we had an overdue break. In my specific case, among other family responsibilities, it meant resting, cooking, and freezing meals for my family.

That joy faded away after a couple of hours. Around 2:00 p.m., the administrator gathered us and invited people to volunteer on Sunday in Building 1. He stated that they needed an extra help due to the large numbers of orders coming in over the weekend. Given that Saturday was already declared off in Building 2, many people signed up for Sunday, also motivated by the promised $150 bonus.

"The bonus will be given for three consecutive Sundays," the administrator said. I guess he didn't want to scare workers by mentioning at that time that they would be required to work every weekend till peak season was over.

A Warehouse II associate had already hinted to me that the hectic schedule would go on till January. I declined the offer. Having that weekend off was more important to me than anything else, including the mighty dollar. To our great surprise, after the administrator left, our dear manager changed her mind and made that Saturday a mandatory workday. As result, some people who had signed up on the volunteer sheet for Sunday went back and crossed off their names.

The coming week was supposed to be eight-hour shifts, but the manager kept imposing mandatory ten-hours, even on Saturday. On Friday when workers were asked to sign up on the volunteer sheet, again, most declined. What puzzles me in all of this mess is that we were treated like robots that are plugged into outlets and never run out of energy. People declined to volunteer even with bonus incentives because they were worn out from working long hours with only Sunday off. The administration's inhumane reaction to that was to make Sunday mandatory too. What the hell? Given that I was already exhausted, I did not see myself surviving three or more weeks of work without a break. Not to mention that I normally go to church on Sundays. This was too much of a demand, since I was already giving six days of my week for the work. I therefore called the agency representative and announced my resignation. The coming Saturday was going to be my last day of work in Warehouse II.

On that Friday, the manager selected some of us and asked us to go directly to Building 1 the next day. We arrived at 5:00 a.m., as requested. A colleague of ours in Building 2, who was sent there a couple of weeks ago to help out, saw us and shouted out loud, "Welcome to hell, ladies! Too much overtime and you won't have anything; taxes will take it away," he added.

They were required to work a minimum of ten to twelve hours per shift for a very long time and were so exhausted that they couldn't help it anymore. However, they had to come to work in order to keep their jobs and be able to pay their bills. I could see that they walked with a dejected spirit and sadness. In that business-to-business department, employees had to walk all shift long, picking phones that were to be packed and shifted by another department. They walked restlessly for about ten to fifteen miles per shift. A computer monitor that depicted the performance of associates or pickers indicated that the average performance was in the red zone, at about 68 percent in work productivity. "How did the administration expect high performance under such conditions?" I asked myself. As long as I worked in Building 1 that day, that average performance never improved, and the poor associates had to go without a day off for many more weeks.

What is this if not a slavery mentality? The work for which we came in that day ran out at 1:30 p.m., which set off a strong reaction in one of us. She expressed her frustration, bitterness, and anger.

Couldn't she have sent us here yesterday to get this done? This is our regular job, and we had spent the whole day yesterday over there (Building 2) doing nothing.

In fact, that Friday they spent time putting lithium battery awareness labels on shipping bags. This was one of the things we did during our special hours. She could have spared us from coming in that Saturday. "Oh my God, abuse of power," we concluded. This sort of animosity had taken deep root in the Warehouse II management system. The bosses never showed any consideration or respect toward employees, as far as I could tell. We were told that when the nearby General Electric building burned down to ashes, the authorities asked every industry around the area to shut down for a while for employee safety. All of the other companies reportedly observed that request except Warehouse II. In addition, they kept working during inclement weather, even giving points to employees who were late due to bad road conditions.

What is the problem here?
Some managers in industries want to be bossy and do not weigh the consequences of their actions. I have a friend who is employed in an industry. When the manager wanted to change her work schedule, she pleaded that her current work schedule was well suited for family responsibilities because it allowed her to pick up her kids from school after work. The manager bluntly replied, "I understand

that you have family responsibilities, but you must understand that I have a business to run." Really!

When employees are frustrated and cannot balance their work schedules with family responsibilities, they either neglect families for the sake of bills or have no other choice but to quit. As a result, managers sometimes find themselves in a stressful situation because they can't find enough workers to cover a whole shift. Their easy, quick solution, in general, is to callously overburden the employees at hand. This puts those employees in a very stressful and desperate situation by being forced to work too hard and/or too long in order to reach the company's goals. The tasks of absentee employees are evenly divided among those who are present, but the associated income is not transferred to those overwhelmed by the extra load.

My journey in nursing homes was quite different. It was greatly exciting when I was offered a position in that industry. I opted for weekend shifts only, due to family responsibilities. Being a certified nursing assistant (CNA) was the right job for me at that time because I could hold a full-time weekend position and still be there for our kids during weekdays, while my husband could take over on weekends. During the interview, I was given the opportunity to choose a schedule either from 7:00 a.m. to 11:00 p.m. (first and second shifts) or from 3:00 p.m. to 7:00 a.m. (second and third shifts). The first schedule fit me well because I could at least have some night sleep between shifts. I was very blessed to find the first option still open. The colleagues who were given the second schedule went through hard times. They could not get enough sleep. After working for sixteen hours, from Saturday afternoon to Sunday morning, they left the floor at 7:00 a.m. only to be back at 3:00 p.m. for another sixteen hours (Sunday afternoon to Monday morning). Given the driving time back and forth, some of them barely had three hours of sleep between their two shifts. One of our colleagues holding that schedule unfortunately lived an hour and a half away. After a couple of months, she was exhausted, fell asleep on her way home one day, and hit the highway curve and went off the road. Glory to God, it was only her car that was damaged beyond repair, and she came out without a scratch. A couple of months later, another colleague, also under that schedule, expressed his frustration and told me that he did not realize at first what he was signing up for. That schedule caused many problems in his life, and shortly after that encounter, he quit. He was a student struggling between school and work in order to make his living and better his life. The first schedule was much better than the second but still physically challenging. From my personal experience, every hour above the eight conventional hours of work is stressful to the body. I held that position for three and a half years in the same nursing home, but most colleagues with whom I started quit sooner than that. Some left after a year of struggle; others resisted for a bit more than a year or reached two years.

Chapter 2

The Point System in US Workplaces

In addition to traditional and modern slavery networks, I find hard to comprehend how human beings are treated in various US industries. The slavery mentality still hovers in people's minds, which makes most managers give no value to human beings and use employees as money-making machines to keep the industry functioning. While in traditional slavery, the whip was used as a tool to discipline slaves, industries today use a point system. It is a modern way of whipping employees in order to discipline them and to shatter their dreams of making careers or moving from temporary to permanent positions.

The nursing home where I once worked had an implemented point system as well. During my tenure there, I did not fully comprehend the cruelty of such a system, mostly because I was a weekend warrior, a term used by the company to denote those holding a full-time weekend position. Staying home on weekdays with our unschooled kids protected me from that stumbling block of "the point system." I did not have to worry about calling in when a child became sick or when school closed for inclement weather. For some companies that apply the point system, calling in, leaving early, or coming late to work, regardless of the motive, means banking points; when one reaches the maximum points fixed by the company, termination follows. I am not supporting employees who call in because they partied a lot the previous night. I am instead advocating for parents who have family responsibilities and at times, due to unforeseeable events, have to call in, come late, or leave early. These people should be able to go without being whipped or falling on the stumbling block set before them.

Warehouse II's point system

Warehouse II gave each new employee six points on the first day of work. I was told by a colleague that after ninety days, six more points are given. The maximum points an employee can have is twelve. These twelve points can be earned after six months of perfect attendance. According to the point policy in force, an employee with perfect attendance during a period of ninety days ultimately would be promoted from temporary to hired. Good! However, most people do not have perfect attendance for ninety days, given the harsh working conditions. I have noticed that the winners of this race are mainly employees who find favor in the eyes of bosses, hardworking single employees, and those who no longer have kids at home. What was meant to be a great incentive for hard work has become a stumbling block for many and especially for parents of young kids. A call-in takes away two points from the total points allocated. An employee leaving before lunch loses two points, while punching out after lunch costs one point; a "no call, no show" takes away four points from the offender. In order to gain one point back, you must have perfect attendance for ninety straight days of work.

One day during my first week of work in Warehouse II, after arriving at 5:00 a.m. as requested by the manager, we quickly ran out of work and were sent to Building 1 for the rest of the day. I met a wonderful and hardworking mother of a toddler who had a broken heart mingled with hope. I was assigned to her for training in what was called the business to business department. She was proud of herself, her dedication, and her hard work. Under her circumstances she was able to work overtime. Hearing her talk about overtime at this point in my tenure there resonated well with me. I did not know at this time that some companies made overtime mandatory. She was only two points away from being hired.

Everything had gone well when she started in Warehouse II almost two years earlier, until one morning, while coming to work, she was the victim of a hit and run accident. As a result, she was forced to stay home for a couple of days, and the point system dragged her to the bottom of the pit. She had worked hard and had gained all of her points back except for two. Most parents in that situation would not be able to catch up with those last two points. Ever. She needed six months of perfect attendance in order to waive the two points and be eligible to move from temporary to permanent employee. She had hope; six months of perfect attendance did not seem impossible or too far away. She had done it before and knew she could do it again. I can still remember her repeating to herself over and over, "I am two points away from being hired." One could tell she was impatient to get hired but very excited about her future situation as a permanent worker. She had reason to be proud of herself. Parents sometimes have to deal with unexpected circumstances such as a child's sudden illness, or a school calling parents to pick up their sick child during work hours. In addition, a child may get in trouble, requiring parental intervention, or school could open late or close early due to inclement weather or any other issue. These unforeseeable events force parents to either leave work early, arrive late to work, or, in some cases, even to call in. Unfortunately, most workplaces like Warehouse II literally refuse to accommodate parents who fall on the stumbling block of "the point system." They are tagged with poor attendance and are on the way to quitting, or worse, getting fired.

On that same day, while I was still training under her care, the staffing agency representative gave her very sad news, which brought her to tears. Her request for a shift change was denied for a third time with no explanation. In fact, she had requested to move from the first shift to the night shift because of some changes in her life; she wanted to stay home with her baby during the daytime, and her mother would spend nights with the child while she worked.

"You would be a great asset for night shift, for they need people," a manager in Building 1 had told her.

"Why did she deny my request for the third time?" she asked the staffing representative, who had no clue.

"She didn't say anything," he replied.

A few hours later, my trainer of the day met a coworker who apparently was her friend and told him in tears, "She denied my request again."

"What did she say this time?" the man asked.

"Nothing," she replied.

Her main place of work was in fact Building 2. She took refuge in Building 1 because her relationship with Building 2's manager had deteriorated after she complained about some inappropriate actions with the manager covering up someone's poor attendance. That employee regularly arrived about an hour late under the watch of the manager, and my trainer quickly found herself overloaded with work that was supposed to have been performed by two people. She was then working in Building 1 but still under the authority of Building 2's manager. Denying this request may have been a way to remind her that, although she worked in Building 1, the other manager still had power over her. What a heartless way to shatter someone's dream! Now with a desperate and hopeless situation at hand, tears kept running down her cheeks whenever she tried to explain her unfortunate situation to a colleague. She was being forced to quit her job, she told us with a dejected spirit. I do not know the end of her story. However, I hope that her request was finally granted and that she did not have to quit her job because of one person's meanness.

Warehouse III's Point System

My shift in Warehouse III was supposed to be from 7:00 a.m. to 7:30 p.m., Saturday through Monday. From my past experience working in warehouses, I knew that it wouldn't be an easy task but had no choice, like many other people in financial distress. After the second fifteen-minute break, which took place at 3:00 p.m. on day 1, the manager summoned us for a meeting.

"An important load of orders came in around two o'clock," he told us and added that we could stay till 9:00 p.m. in order to process everything before leaving. Staying till 9:00 p.m. was therefore mandatory. Nobody was supposed to leave the floor until the shift leader gave permission. To back this instruction, he threatened to give three points to anyone who left the floor early. At the time this news came, I was already having sore feet and back pain; despite the pain, the fear of three points made me stay till the end (8:30 p.m.). I was not able to stand up straight at the end of that shift. I came in the next day with apprehension, fearing another mandatory overtime, which unfortunately came to pass. As a result of the mandatory overtime, many people did not come in the next day. We were short-handed. During the first break, the absence system sheet was distributed (see table 1 below).

Table 1: Warehouse III Absence Point System	
Issue/Item	Point Assigned
Late < 15 minutes	0.5
Late > 15 minutes < 1 hour	0.75
Late > 1 hour	1
Unapproved Absence (per day)	1
Three days or more with doctor's note	1
No call, no show	5
Unapproved early departure	3

Consequences	Point Level
Documented verbal warning	2
Written warning	4
Final written warning	6
Termination	8

Reduction of points	Time Frame
Issues/Items and associated points	Expire one year from item date

Table 1 *(continued)*

1 point reduction for perfect attendance	Each consecutive three-month period of no lateness, unapproved absence, or early departure (no overlapping months). Absence that falls under state or federal mandated LOA laws will not be included. Absence that results from work-related accident will not be included.

One shift leader voiced concerns regarding surgical cases. Given that after surgery, the patient would likely stay home for more than three days, how would they address such an issue?

This was her concern. She promised herself to put it on the table during their meeting with the manager. The above chart indicates that an employee who showed up but could not work the whole twelve hours scheduled was three times more severely punished compared to another who, for whatever reason, decided to call in. In addition, if a sick employee missed twenty-four days of work, he/she was ultimately terminated, according to the above point policy. This was a better situation than we had in Warehouse I but was still unfair. Why should people devote their lives to a company that would trash them just for getting sick? Actually, one could become sick as a result of poor working conditions and a hectic schedule. By 9:00 a.m. that day, all of the previous day's pain was already back and increased with every tick of the clock. Around 3:00 p.m. I saw a lady leaping in pain like I was. She also had probably declined pain pills or did not remember to carry some with her. We were three in our team. One of us had some pain pills and offered them to both of us, since she saw us struggling. As usual, I declined the offer, as did the other colleague, who at some point couldn't help it anymore and disappeared for about thirty to forty-five minutes. Fortunately for him, the shift leader and the manager did not notice his absence. Giving my own struggle, I understood his attitude and wished I had the courage to enjoy such a break. Around 5:00 p.m., as I was going to the restroom, I noticed my shoelace was loose. I tried to bend to tie it but realized that I couldn't do so. I felt an excruciating pain in my back due to prolonged standing with little walking. The shift leader caught me stuck, halfway bent, struggling to get to my shoelace.

"Are you OK?" he asked me.

"I can't tie my shoelace," I replied, adding, "My back is in so much pain that I can't bend to my shoes."

"I will do it for you," he replied.

As he was talking, he bent and tied my shoelace. I expressed my gratitude. At 7:30 p.m., I noticed that everybody was focused on their tasks. Nobody seemed to notice that the shift had come to an end. I was very alert because I had been waiting eagerly for that time to arrive. The pain I felt made me check the time very often. For me, 7:30 p.m. couldn't pass unnoticed, and finally it was there. But it looked like I was the only one keeping my eyes on the clock. Even the other lady on our team wasn't surprised by the situation. She had been working there for a month and knew that, like the previous day, nobody could leave unless all orders were processed. I drew her attention to the fact that it was already 7:30 p.m. She went and asked someone about the load of undone work. That person did not know either.

I realized that pickers were still picking. "But for how long?" I asked myself. The previous day, after 7:30 p.m., they told us that there were about two hundred items to process, going from picking, packing, and shipping. That day they left us uninformed, and by then I couldn't even stand up straight. My back pain and sore feet were over-whelming. Despite the discomfort, I armed myself with patience; after all, I did not want to bank three points after a long day of hard work. At 8:30 p.m., it did not seem to me that the supervisors were anywhere close to ending the shift. I immediately understood that I could not consider a long-term career in such an environment. I set myself up to go home despite the three unfair points. I went to the shift leader and asked him to clock me out. That system was set up in such a way that only the shift leader could clock employees out on a computer. He indeed refused to do so, saying that nobody was supposed to leave unless the work was done for the day. I reminded him that on the previous day, we were told that the shift might end at 9:00 p.m., and such an announcement had not been made that day.

"Why shouldn't I leave?" I asked him.

He asked me to go back to my station and keep working until he said it was over.

"For how long?" I asked him, and added, "I could strive for another thirty minutes, but you are not giving me any hope." He told me that he wasn't sure how long it would be and sent me to talk to the manager.

At the meeting with the manager, I told him that I wanted to leave, but the shift leader sent me to him.

"You don't have to work here," he replied.

I wasn't shocked by such an attitude. In fact, when he had announced the day before that we would work till 9:00 p.m., I had exclaimed out loud, "Am I a slave?" The lady who stood near me heard that and moved to another spot. She surely must have reported that to him.

"I know I do not have to work here, and that's why I want to leave, regardless of the three points," I answered.

"The hierarchy gave us strict orders not to let anybody leave unless all orders are processed," he insisted.

"What if it doesn't get finished? Are we going to spend the night here?"

He refused to answer that question.

Then I added that the shift leader did not tell us how much time we still needed to complete the orders.

"My computer is telling me that it's about twenty to thirty minutes and everything will be done," he told me.

"OK, I can struggle for another twenty or thirty minutes," I replied.

Thank God, it lasted about the time range he gave me. I left work thinking I would be back the next day but kept wondering what would happen if my back did not get better overnight. At this place of work, one was not given a chance to leave the floor early, even while in trouble. The punishment for leaving early was three times more severe than calling in. I opted to call in the third day. It was a smart decision because my back pain could significantly worsen on the third day of struggle. I was still in pain on Monday despite calling in but felt much better on Tuesday. As I was planning to request a schedule change, I realized that it wasn't worth asking because the weekly schedule went from Tuesday to Friday. If I couldn't stand for the three days I was given at first, how could I stand for four? Given the loopholes in their point system, I realized that if I worked Saturdays and Mondays while calling in on Sundays, I could at least keep those two days for eight weeks before being terminated.

Glory to God, I never went back. He opened another door that same week in a memory care retirement community. This was the only place of work I encountered where a mother could leave early because of a child's sickness or arrive late because of some family problems, without been punished. Thumbs-up! During my experience at Warehouse III, I questioned some associates about how they were dealing with the working conditions. The answers were with pain pills, a back brace, a knee brace, and pain patches. Is it not possible to improve working conditions so that employees do not have to use those survival tools? Yes we can!

I had a different experience with Warehouse IV. At this place I sensed a flavor of human dignity and respect, to some extent. The first shift normally started at 6:30 a.m. In our first week, a warning was given that we would gear up to 5:30 a.m. when a large number of orders came in. This made a lot more sense to me. In addition, mandatory overtime and the normal shift never went beyond nine hours of daily work. In meetings, our hard work was acknowledged, and the administration admitted the physically challenging nature of tasks, encouraging people to give their best. As I was holding a temporary position, I worked there for two weeks and walked away pain free.

Chapter 3

Poor Working Conditions and Hectic Schedules Come with Great Health and Social Consequences

Under hectic schedules at Warehouse II or elsewhere, most people use pain pills and energy drinks to strengthen their bodies. In addition, employees are exposed to a lot of stress at work. All of these parameters are proven risk factors for many diseases. I personally experienced the downhill effect of energy drinks. That is essentially why I declined the offer in Warehouse II. After working thirty-two hours a weekend in the nursing home for more than a year, my body started slowing down; the energy I had on day one was gone, and it became extremely hard for me to complete those thirty-two hours in two days. In order to boost my strength, I took a sip of coffee each workday, although with a fearful mind, for I had been told that coffee is a risk factor for some cancers. But I had no choice, because I needed something to keep me awake. Sunday, especially on second shift, was when I felt like I couldn't make it. But by the grace of God, I kept pushing forward, since I needed the money.

One day in the break room, I saw a colleague with a can of soft drink on which "energy drink" was written, among other information. Wow!

"That's what I need. Where did you get it?" I asked her.

"In any store you can find it," she replied.

As a foreigner trying to find my way in an unfamiliar country, I did not know such drinks existed. A drink that could boost my strength! The next time we went shopping, I wasted no time grabbing a few bottles. What an easy solution to my problem! From that time on, I made sure to carry one in my lunch box. What puzzled me was that the list of ingredients read "no sugar added," but it was awfully sweet. I then added some water to dilute it to my taste. Apart from its taste, the expected result was there. I could enjoy my work full of energy and did not at any time question the safety of the drink.

A couple of months later, I was sipping my energy drink in the break room when another colleague stepped in and looked shocked.

"I can't believe you drink that!" he exclaimed.

Just hearing him talk that way, I felt like I was doing some horrible thing.

"What is wrong with this? It boosts my energy," I replied.

"It will increase your blood pressure if you do not stop," he warned me.

"I did not know it was dangerous," I replied and rushed to empty the rest in the sink.

After the break I rushed to the nursing station and got my blood pressure checked. It was 120/75, still in a good range but higher than 100/59, which had been my reading for many years. As long as can I remember, my blood pressure was always stable at 100/59. I could have easily slipped into the prehypertension or hypertension stage if that colleague had not warned me about the danger of energy drinks. Other factors could have played a role in the shift in my blood pressure as well. But who knows?

After a while I met the colleague who introduced me to that product and asked if she knew how dangerous the drink was. She in fact knew about this, but claimed she had been drinking it for a long time and still was doing just fine. Even if she felt fine at the time, she was, unfortunately, exposing herself to the danger of high blood pressure, which is the so-called "silent killer." I only understood this threat later, after I had left that nursing home, so I did not have the opportunity to raise her awareness about the risk she was running. Other risk factors will be highlighted below.

Energy Drinks: Risk factors for Multiple Diseases

Many scientific studies have highlighted the deleterious effects of energy drinks. In their article entitled "Energy

Drink: Health Risk and Toxicity," Gunja and Brown demonstrated that energy drinks are a risk factor for health problems such as hallucination, seizure, cardiac ischemia, and gastrointestinal upset (Gunja and Brown 2012). Furthermore, they stressed that even small amounts of caffeine (50 mg), which is the usual amount in energy drinks, can cause tachycardia and agitation (Gunja and Brown 2012). Wanjek, on the Live Science web page, described a crossover study conducted in twenty-five healthy patients in which each individual received a can of energy drink; blood pressure was measured before and after drink consumption. The results showed that after taking the drink, systolic blood pressure was 3 percent higher than it had been before (Wanjek 2015). According to Zeratsky, individuals exposed to energy drinks may experience nervousness, irritability, insomnia, rapid heartbeat, and increased blood pressure, due to high amounts of caffeine (Zeratsky 2015). Some of the symptoms mentioned above have short-term latency (e.g., dizziness, irritability) while others have long-term latency. Therefore, not having symptoms immediately after consuming the drink doesn't mean everything is fine. For example, cardiac arrest is commonly known as a silent killer. Industries should not be concerned solely with profit and jeopardize the health of their employees with burdensome schedules, which force them to take these dangerous beverages in order to boost their energy.

Zeratsky offers a healthy way to overcome tiredness, stating that good sleep, regular exercise, and a healthy diet are appropriate means to boost energy (Zeratsky 2015). Awesome! These are great suggestions. From my personal experience, individuals working eight-hour shifts may not need energy stimulants or boosters. However, an extra two to four hours or more constitutes the toughest work time. A healthy diet is difficult to implement with a lean, slavery-like income. It is also difficult to have good sleep habits with a hectic schedule like the one I had. For most people, and especially parents, the end of a work shift means the beginning of another shift at home with all sorts of family responsibilities, which might include picking up a child from daycare, waiting for other children at the bus stop, shopping, cooking, doing laundry, housekeeping, and the list goes on and on. One can hardly find time to get appropriate amounts of rest in such conditions. With mandatory overtime from Monday through Sunday, one is bound to go to bed late and still get up as early as 2:00 a.m., 3:00 a.m., or 4:00 a.m., for a long period of time. Under such hectic schedules, most people have no choice but to go for fast foods, which have been identified as risk factors for health problems such as obesity, type 2 diabetes, and cardiovascular disease, in order to lighten the burden of all the responsibilities listed above. In addition, individuals using energy drinks at work often need those stimulants to boost energy at home as well. As a consequence, most individuals consume as many stimulants as they can afford, running the risk of excessive caffeine and/or sugar in the body, while dealing with hectic schedules, which could bring even more complicated health issues.

Stress

The work environment described above exposes employees to work-related stress. Some workers, voluntarily and for many reasons, including low income, take long hourly shifts seven days a week for a very long period of time. However, when employers make overtime mandatory, it becomes problematic. The stress that accompanies mandatory overtime is higher than that endured in normal circumstances, when someone acts with free will. Dr. Goldberg asserted that stress can have a positive or negative effect on the body. It becomes harmful when someone is trapped in prolonged challenges with no room for relief or relaxation (Goldberg 2014). He added that in such situations, the victim becomes overworked, leading to the generation of stress-related tension (Goldberg 2014). Most individuals under stress use drugs as a tool for relaxation. Unfortunately, these drugs tend to maintain the body in a stressed state, which comes with many health consequences (Goldberg 2014). Physical symptoms of stress are high blood pressure, lack of sleep, headache, chest pain, and upset stomach. Stress is also recognized as a risk factor for conditions such as heart disease, diabetes, depression, asthma, anxiety, and arthritis (Goldberg 2014). Goldberg found that 43 percent of all adults are in distress due to stress-related adverse health effects, while 75 percent to 90 percent of all hospital visits are prompted by stress-related sicknesses (Goldberg 2014). Moreover, Goldberg found that people exposed to chronic stress are more likely to develop an emotional disorder about 50 percent of the time if they do not seek care (Goldberg 2014).

Pain

On a shift lasting ten to twelve hours or more, standing in one spot, bending, or walking about ten to fifteen miles is extremely tiresome and very painful. This pain results from muscle injury caused by excessive strain on a particular muscle or group of muscles, ligaments, or tendons. Companies, as mentioned above, provide pain pills to employees, although some employees prefer to bring their own. However, using them continually comes with consequences. Indeed, in the long run, the body gets used to pills, and they can no longer deliver the expected results. After the stage of dependency, the user would have to move to a stronger medicine (e.g., narcotics), or worse, illicit drugs. No wonder so many people are addicted to narcotics in the United States.

When workers have prolonged hardship with all the health consequences highlighted above, they find themselves in a vicious cycle with no way out. For example, when they can't sleep anymore due to excessive caffeine from energy drinks, they lean on sleeping pills in order to get some rest. In the long run, they also become addicted to those pills.

Social Consequences

Given the health consequences of fast food, our family opted to buy fast food only as a reward for good school performance by our kids, in order to stimulate hard work because they love fast food. Most kids actually do. As we have four school-age kids, we used to eat fast food four times a year—that is, when one of our kids was selected student of the month. During the time that I worked in warehouses, we ate more fast food than ever. In my struggle to keep my job, family responsibilities were slipping through my hands, and I could see myself bringing the stress of hard work home, which expressed itself as rising anger. How many homes are turned upside down when husbands and wives are oppressed at work with harsh schedules? What happens when a spouse, and especially the wife, is no longer able to respond to her husband's desire under such hectic schedules? What was supposed to be a solution to financial distress turns into a stumbling block for couples because some people have turned their fellow human beings into money-making robots.

Chapter 4

Slavery-Like Income

The only reward slaves received from their masters for intense and prolonged labor was food. They had no future but to labor for their masters till death came or they were sold as a property to other masters. Today's minimum wage and incomes slightly above it can be compared to the food slaves were given: income that satisfies only one's stomach! No one earning the minimum wage or slightly above can dream of owning a home, planning for retirement, or affording adequate health (or any) insurance. Many workers whose hourly income is between ten and thirteen dollars may be able to afford insurance for themselves but not for their offspring. In addition, they cannot financially support their kids as college students. The list goes on. Even with mandatory overtime, life is still tough for employees with an hourly income around the minimum wage.

Let's do some math. In a typical hectic week, an employee in Warehouse II working ten hours each day (Monday through Sunday) takes home about $600 after taxes, for those without company benefits (health, dental, and vision insurance, and/or retirement plan). Let's assume that his/her weekly income remains the same throughout the year. This gives an estimate of $2,600 a month or $31,200 a year. Table 2 depicts an estimation of the average annual expenditures of Americans in 2014.

Table 2: Average Annual Expenditure, 2014	
Food	**6,759**
Food at home	3,971
Food away from home	2,787
House	17,798
Shelter	**10,491**
Owned	6,149
Rented	3,631
Apparel and services	1,786
Transportations	**9,073**
Fuel	2,468
Insurance	1,112
Health care	4,290
Health insurance	2,868
Entertainment	2,728
Cash contributions	1,788
Personal insurance and pension	5,726
All other expenditures	**3,548**

Source: Adapted from US Bureau of Labor Statistics (2014)

The amounts highlighted in the chart total $29,871, absorbing almost all the estimated annual income of $31,200. It's clear that many other needs were not included. No wonder Americans live on credit card debts. The wage statistics for 2014 released by the Social Security Administration indicated that 51.44 percent of Americans' yearly income is below $30,000 (Social Security Administration 2016). In addition, the Census Bureau revealed that in 2014, 36.6 percent of full-time year-round workers earned below $35,000. Among them, 5.9 percent had an income below $15,000; 14 percent earned between $15,000 and $25,000; and 16.7 percent had an income range of $25,000–$35,000 (Census Bureau 2014d). These individuals work hard throughout the year, some with mandatory overtime, yet are not able to afford a decent life. The broken system has shattered their dreams and kept them, for the most part, forever in poverty. The only things reminding them of their hard work are lack of sleep, untreated stress, back pain, sore feet, unpaid credit cards, high blood pressure, heart diseases, and diabetes. Most of these people are poor, but not poor enough to qualify for welfare or safety net programs. Why should the government provide extra financial support to full-time employees anyway? The threshold of poverty as defined by the Census Bureau is very low, in order to include all households in need (see table 3 below).

Table 3:—Poverty thresholds for 2015 by size of family and number of related children under 18 years old

Size of family unit	Related children under 18 years								
	None	One	Two	Three	Four	Five	Six	Seven	Eight or more
One person (unrelated individual)...									
Under 65 years...	12,331								
65 years and over...	11,367								
Two people...									
Householder under 65 years...	15,871	16,337							
Householder 65 years and over...	14,326	16,275							

Table 3 (*continued*)

Size of family unit	Related children under 18 years								
	None	One	Two	Three	Four	Five	Six	Seven	Eight or more
Three people...	18,540	19,078	19,096						
Four people...	24,447	24,847	24,036	24,120					
Five people...	29,482	29,911	28,995	28,286	27,853				
Six people...	33,909	34,044	33,342	32,670	31,670	31,078			
Seven people...	39,017	39,260	38,421	37,835	36,745	35,473	34,077		
Eight people...	43,637	44,023	43,230	42,536	41,551	40,300	38,999	38,668	
Nine people or more...	52,493	52,747	52,046	51,457	50,490	49,159	47,956	47,658	45,822

Source: Adapted from U.S. Census Bureau

Let's consider the poverty threshold for a family of six people (two parents and four kids), which is $31,670 a year, as seen in the table above. As a reminder, this income is the figure before taxes are taken out. With this income, the above household falls into the 2015 tax bracket of $9,225–$37,450, which has a federal tax rate of 15 percent. After deductions and exemptions, this family would pay about $4,000 in income tax to the federal government. The state will take some money, too, according to state tax policies. Let's assume, then, that this family takes home about $27,500 a year. This family qualifies for welfare, which will probably cover food (food stamps) and/or health insurance (Passport for kids and Medicare or Medicaid, depending on age, for parents or guardians). The basic needs of this family will be met.

But let's consider another family of six whose income is just fifty dollars above the yearly $31,670 highlighted above. The additional fifty dollars would disqualify the family from government aid, even though their financial situation does not give them any advantage over the first family. The second family may elect to decline health coverage by their employer in order to maximize their cash flow; even in this case, their weekly take-home pay will be just a couple of dollars more than that of the first family. Many families in this situation, in fact, do decline health coverage and other benefits from their employer such as a 401(k) retirement plan and dental and vision insurance. (The new tax bracket adopted in 2018 brought a 3 percent tax cut for the middle class and below. It provides some additional cash flow but not enough to make a substantial difference in the example here.)

Meanwhile, a family of this size in some US states cannot legally live in a two-bedroom apartment, according to current laws. A three-bedroom rental apartment costs about $1,000 a month in Louisville, Kentucky, for example. Therefore, this family would spend more than one-third of their income just on rent. In addition, they may pay about $400 in monthly health insurance premiums, if they decide to be insured. Some families, despite hard work, live in homes without an air conditioner and/or heating system. It is practically impossible for a family of six to have a decent life with such a slavery-like income. As a consequence, some US families choose to minimize their incomes by only accepting part-time or seasonal jobs in order to remain forever qualified for government aid. A colleague at work recently (2019) was forced to cut her work hours down to thirty-nine every two weeks in order to keep her health insurance. This is so wrong. A better solution could be implemented (see chapter 5). In 2014, 18.5 percent (10,981,679) of US workers holding part-time jobs year-round and 3 percent (2,973,051) of full-time year-round employees were below the poverty level (Census Bureau 2014c). Most of these individuals do not dream big anymore. They find some elusive comfort in that unfortunate situation, and some of those who dare to dream see their dreams shattered.

Shattered Dreams and Hopes for Some Low-Income Individuals in the United States

People respond to hard times and trouble in different ways. Some people resignedly accept the situation and deal with it the best way they can. Others try to escape. Unfortunately, an attempt to escape might bring either complete victory or total chaos, depending on the means and determination, as well as the social, economic, and political circumstances. For example, early slaves could not easily escape because the majority of whites at that time advocated for slavery. Yet as some people realized that it wasn't right to own a human being, they stepped up and helped slaves to escape the tragedy. However, not all oppressed slaves attempted to escape, and not all those who tried to escape freed themselves:

* Some were captured and brought back to their masters.
* Others were drowned in the Ohio River and never experienced their lifelong desired freedom.
* The lucky ones crossed the river successfully to freedom.

Below, I will use these three analogies to describe many Americans, including myself.

My Personal Experience

The United States of America is considered a dream country by many foreigners. When my husband was offered a position in this country in 2006, I knew that doors would be opened for me to further my education and finally get a good job. Before we migrated, I was enrolled in a master's program in finance at the University of Umea (Sweden), where we lived for three and a half years. That was my lifelong dream. After we got married in 2000 and moved to Europe, I was home taking care of our kids but longing to go back to school one day. That year, 2006, was when my dream was about to come true. Unfortunately, we had to migrate to the United States. Still, I wasn't desperate, knowing that the United States is a land of opportunities. I knew that once in the United States, going back to school would not happen overnight, but I was still excited about the multiple opportunities potentially coming my way.

Coming from a poor family, I did not want to forget my origin. On the one hand, I wanted to reach out and help my siblings and relatives. Therefore, finding a job (any job) as soon as possible was critical. On the other hand, I longed to go back to school, given the difficulties of finding a good job with a degree only from my country of origin, Cameroon. Not only that, but I had lost my enthusiasm and love for marketing while in Europe, when I saw companies using naked people in ads for cars, tea, and anything. Sending our kids to daycare was not an option, given the high costs. We figured out that almost all my income from "odd" jobs would have to be spent paying for daycare services, and there was really no point in doing so. After giving it deep thought, a nursing assistant position sounded appropriate because I could hold a full-time weekend position and be there for our kids as well on weekdays, while my husband could take over on weekends.

In the meantime, I was working on taking the Graduate Record Exam (GRE). Given that my education was mainly in French, it took me two years to prepare for the GRE. Thank God, my score amazed even English-speaking Cameroonian friends. With the GRE completed, I was ready and eager to make my dream come true. My husband wanted me to wait till the then-youngest kid went to school—that is, 2013—so that I could freely attend lectures without worrying about daycare. By that time, however, God had blessed us with four beautiful babies. I had been waiting since 2000 to go back to school and couldn't wait much longer. Therefore, I decided to take online courses; I graduated on August 25, 2013, with a master's in public health (MPH) degree from a university based in Minnesota. Holding a full-time job while enrolled in a full-time graduate program, coupled with four kids and family responsibilities, was a nightmare, but the hope for a better future kept pushing me forward. I knew the time to finally breathe was at hand.

All of my excitement, joy, and hope quickly faded away when I started applying for jobs. With my MPH degree, the first focus was on government jobs. I quickly noticed that I failed to fulfill a major requirement for all government jobs: accreditation! Your degree program must have been accredited. I rushed online to check whether the MPH program I took was accredited. Unfortunately, it wasn't. In fact, after spending three weeks in the MPH program, a friend of my husband's asked me to ensure that the MPH program and the university itself were accredited. Although the school was indeed accredited, the program wasn't. The school instead had a pending application for accreditation for the MPH program. He kindly asked me to withdraw from the program because according to him, chances were that I would never work with an unaccredited degree. I had declined his suggestion, hoping that by the end of the two years, the university would be granted accreditation for its MPH program. After sending out job applications for two years, I never had an interview. It was then that another friend of ours bluntly said that companies generally disregard degrees earned in for-profit universities. What a shocking discovery!

Why, then, does the government provide tuition to students to enroll in such universities without being willing to hire them and knowing that the vast majority of companies will not employ them either? How many students in this country fall into this trap and end up with a large amount of school debt with no hope of repayment? According to the U.S. Census Bureau's statistics, 10.5 percent (6,281,106) of US citizens holding some college or associate degree and 4.5 percent (2,735,265) with a bachelor's degree or higher are below the poverty level (Census Bureau 2014c).

In the United States, there are a handful of poor individuals who seem to be content with the poor conditions offered and do not try to escape. Some others, including myself, have tried to escape poverty through education. Unfortunately, the cruel system put into place has caught us and drowned us into poverty with little or no hope of escape. Some of us have been lucky enough to graduate but will never get a job, while others stepped out with no degree. People in the third analogy mentioned above are those who were alert and chose accredited programs or were lucky enough to be employed. Individuals attending for-profit universities who already hold a position and are just seeking promotion are also more likely to profit from their training. However, it is nearly impossible to start a new career with an unaccredited degree.

Another point raised by some is that for-profit universities provide an education of questionable quality. My personal experience corroborates that claim. In a biostatistics class, we had an online discussion board where individual essays were posted, and each student was required to read at least two contributions from colleagues and ask questions or comment. Another board was set up for any other questions related to difficult assignments, and students were required to help their peers solve those problems. I was personally shocked that the lecturer never on any occasion stepped in to help us solve those problems. I did not understand if it was the university's policy to let students help each other in finding solutions without the lecturer's intervention or whether the particular lecturer just lacked the necessary knowledge and understanding to help out, leaving us to ourselves. After I answered questions from some students in the first week, my peers quickly noticed that I had a better understanding of that subject and asked me for answers, which I joyfully provided. The questions above our level of understanding were simply left unanswered. At the end of that class, I refused to take the evaluation survey because I was greatly disappointed. However, I was even more shocked when students praised him/ her as a great professor on the board. They were just overjoyed for passing that class because, as many of them said, it was very stressful.

Another disappointment took place during my practicum. When I arrived at my practicum site, the first thing they asked was what software I was familiar with.

"SPSS," I told them.

"We use SAS," the lady retorted.

The copy of the SPSS software we used in the biostatistics class more than a year earlier had expired. The lady promised to find a copy of the SPSS software for me but did not keep her promise. I quickly figured out that Microsoft Excel would be my way out. Excel was an easy substitute because of the type of data at hand. However, one of our classmates had a very shameful experience. Her practicum site put the SPSS software at her disposal, but she could not input the data properly. She sent me an email asking for help.

"How do you input data in SPSS?" she asked, surely after recalling how helpful I had been during the biostatistics class.

Unfortunately, I was unable to help her. After giving it some thought, I figured out that we were not taught how to input data in SPSS. In the class, data were already input, and we only imported them into SPSS on computers and performed the requested analysis. They taught us all sorts of variables, including string, numerical, and ordinal variables, but never gave us any practical problem that required filling up the SPSS data sheet. I felt very sorry for her and for all of us. I replied to her, explaining my inability to help. It was only then that I realized how I would have been in great disgrace by showing my inability to use software that I claimed to have mastered. I do not know how the classmate got out of that mess. Since I couldn't help her, it was useless for me to follow up with that case. I guess she did humble herself before her mentor and asked for help. The opportunity to "sell" ourselves turned out to be chaotic for some. At the end of the program, I filled that gap by taking an SPSS online tutorial.

I encountered another issue during the health evaluation class. We were asked to go to a public health center or any health education center in our city to get a project they had launched in the past in order to evaluate it as part of our course. The problem here was that because of privacy and confidentiality concerns, they cannot give you every document that you need for an accurate evaluation.

What I got was very limited. I am grateful, though, that I had something to work on. I strongly believe that, in order to solve this problem, the school should provide the project to the students. No wonder most private employers, as well as the government, do not want to hire students who attended for-profit universities.

But my question remains. Why does the government provide loans to students enrolling in for-profit universities? Why overburden people who are trying to get out of poverty with huge amounts of federal loans, knowing that companies will not be interested in their degree or training? Education aiming at improving the economic situation instead drives people into a slimy pit. Not only do such students remain unemployed or continue with low-income jobs, but they also have a huge loan to repay. I strongly believe that this crisis needs to be addressed. The system should stop making more victims. For-profit universities are out there making money on the backs of the needy. During my first semester at my university, I bought course books either at their library online or Amazon, depending on which offered the best deal. The university quickly noticed I wasn't buying all my books from its and reacted in a smart way. Around the beginning of the third semester, I went on the website to check the list of books and figure out which ones to buy from the university. Unfortunately, I found none. About a week before the beginning of that semester, I sent an email to one of its customer service agents, explaining my problem. I got a stunning response:

"Oh, do not worry about your order placement; it has been already shipped to your address, and you will receive it in a couple of days."

Was this manna from heaven? I asked myself.

When I received my tuition bill for that semester, there was an increase of about $160. I called them and requested an explanation. A lady told me that school fees had been increased. I understood this to mean that the increase was related to the books I received without placing any order. From that time on, they sent me books at the beginning of each semester without being contacted by me.

Hanford (2016) argued that in 2010, 10 percent of all students who enrolled in universities went to for-profit colleges or universities. Among these students, 96 percent took out federal loans compared to only 13 percent of those attending community colleges. Meanwhile, 48 percent and 57 percent of students enrolled in four-year public and non-profit schools, respectively, received government money (Hanford 2016). This stems from the fact that more students who are enrolled in for-profit schools are from poor families and can only afford education through loans. Yet their dreams are shattered. According to Hanford, for-profit universities and colleges collected $32 billion in federal loans and Pell Grants in

2010 (Hanford 2016). The Pell Grants, which is non-reimbursable, represented a small portion of this amount.

Meanwhile, students are required to pay loans back with a significant interest rate of about 6.8 percent for those in graduate studies. Hanford stressed that about half of students holding these loans default on their payments (Hanford 2016). Among them, some have resigned without any degree but are compelled to pay back the loans. These loans keep accruing interest till paid in full; if not paid before then, the debt will be paid from social security wages when people grow old. For low-income folks, the social security wage itself is not consistent and would not be enough to cover all those debts with accrued interest. As a result, some people in their old age will be denied their social security benefit because of useless school loans contracted as youths. I wonder if all these poor students foresee the danger. Suzie Mandy in her talk show once said that no one can get out of repaying school loans by declaring bankruptcy. She urged people to pay off their school loans by all means.

But where will they get the money if no company is willing to hire them? I personally do not enjoy paying interest on credit cards or any other loan. Keeping my full-time job while in school was for that purpose. In September 2011, when I started my MPH program, I was already exhausted from holding down a full-time weekend job as a nursing assistant with family responsibilities, but it did not stop me from pursuing my dream, although it ended up shattered. I dove into the waters with hope that God would not let me drown. In fact, he upheld me throughout that journey. I knew it wouldn't be easy but did not expect it to be as challenging as it was. A full-time job, full-time graduate program, four kids, and family responsibilities were a nightmare to me, and I would not recommend that to anybody. I am so grateful to God that I finished that journey alive. I am even more grateful that I could pay off my school loan without accrued interest. Many people like me have invested that much in vain.

The proposal to reduce funding to for-profit universities has been resisted by for-profit schools' owners and Republicans. The Grand Old Party is quick to fight any social endeavor proposed by the Democratic Party, opposing any resolutions to close loopholes that hinder the emancipation of poor communities in the United States (e.g., wage increases, reduction of funding to for-profit schools). In reality, the Republicans manufacture poverty and want people to remain forever poor with no hope whatsoever and no help from the government. Poverty is willingly constructed in the United States. Hanford stated that, in 2009, CEOs of for-profit schools earned on average $7.3 million, including stocks, options, and bonuses (Hanford 2016). If you look at the salaries of the housekeeping staff that year in the same companies, you'll realize that they were barely putting food on the table with seven dollars or $8.50 hourly gross income, little or no health insurance, no 401(k) retirement plans and no means to send kids to colleges. The list goes on and on.

Throughout my education in my native Cameroon, I studied the downside of capitalism but never had a chance to experience it. Capitalism is commonly known as a system in which the poor are doomed to remain poor, while the rich are in the position to get even richer. People who support capitalism stress that the key to success is hard work. However, my personal experience in the odd job field has proven that this is just a fallacy in the capitalist world. The government, through school loans, fills up the pockets of for-profit universities at the expense of poor students, who in this way are abused and rejected. What is left for such individuals is to try their luck in another school, therefore sinking even deeper in debt, but making sure that they enroll this time in accredited programs. Alternatively, they could desperately go from odd job to odd job for the rest of their lives, bound to deal with awful and unjust mandatory overtimes, which push them to behaviors that put them at risk for various chronic diseases. This needs to be addressed.

Chapter 5

Some Solutions

With such a problem at hand, people should not sit back waiting for Congress to pass bills that will improve their life conditions. These politicians swim in six-figure salaries, while CEOs and board members fly in seven-figure salaries in addition to multimillion-dollar bonuses. At the same time, the very people who carry the companies on their shoulders cannot afford a decent house, have poor health insurance policies with high deductibles, and cannot save for retirement. I was shocked when I saw a man in his late sixties or early seventies holding a house-keeping position in one of the warehouses I worked for. It is easy to speculate that he had been doing similar jobs his whole life; however, his income level did not allow him to invest in retirement. Because of slavery-like wages, his social security income was probably too little to live on, given inflation. How many seniors still struggle for their living? According to the Census Bureau, 9.4 percent of Americans aged sixty-five and older were below poverty level or poor in 2014 (Census Bureau 2014b).

Senators and representatives cannot provide the best solution. The late Thomas Sankara, a former president of Burkina Faso, once stressed that the morality of the rich is different from that of the poor. That said, a congressman cannot sit in a mansion and understand poverty the same way that poor people can. That is why I respectfully disagreed with Hillary Clinton's proposal to fight for $12.10 as the minimum wage if she was elected in 2016. The $15 hourly wage suggested by Bernie Sanders would have been acceptable if it was take-home income, meaning that companies would automatically tap into their overflow resources to cover employees' income taxes or at least provide full health insurance from the overflow. The latter is possible in a situation where hospital costs are controlled by the government. None of these candidates succeeded in 2016. We know who did. In the present system, where income is taxable and, for some people, coupled with health insurance premiums, an acceptable minimum wage would be around $20 an hour.

In order to accomplish this, CEOs and board members should simply waive a small portion of their multimillion-dollar bonuses. Some people argue that raising income ships jobs overseas. However, if the raise is coupled with penalties on companies that attempt to take jobs away, as advocated by President Donald Trump, the problem more likely will be solved. Alternatively, companies could include all employees in sharing the bonus. I am not talking about the $50 or $100 gift cards that some companies give their employees around Thanksgiving and Christmas. It should be a substantial amount, in order to make workers feel rewarded and appreciated for their hard work. In addition, company leaders should be willing not to increase or double the price of goods in the market. My suggestion does not add any additional burden to the company. For example, if a company used to pay its CEO $5 million a year, let that company pay him $4 million and divide the difference among the lower class. Alternatively, a company could take a small portion from each board member's salary to make up the million dollars. These are costs that the company already bears but have chosen to put in the hands of only a few people.

Good incomes or salaries attract workers. During peak season, some employers add up to four dollars per hour to their regular wage to stimulate employment. It is ludicrous for workers to have minimal or no health insurance coverage because of low incomes and yet have to pay hospital bills out of pocket because of the so-called "deductible." The deductible directs the patient's eyes away from the insurer every time he/she is lost in the midst of thousands of dollars of health care bills. It is a bizarre situation in which the insurer tells the patients, "You pay the bill, not us." Hospital bills at times could equal the income from four months or even more of hard work for low-income individuals, sometimes for a hospital visit lasting only three to five hours. Employers are supposed to increase wages at least on a yearly basis. Because of greed, the rate applied for an income raise is ridiculous. I started working in a nursing home at eleven dollars an hour. After three years of work, my income was adjusted to $11.55 an hour, while inflation was three to five times this rate. Income in the United States goes up at the speed of a turtle, while inflation increases exponentially. Inflation in the United States could be partially explained by increased gas prices, which drive retail stores to disproportionately increase costs. However, when gas prices go down, the same stores do not adjust their prices accordingly, therefore making huge profits. Thumbs-up to some stores like Aldi that do not cheat customers in that way. They usually allow their prices to fluctuate with gas prices.

There is a great imbalance in living costs and income between those in the middle class and those on slavery-like incomes. President Barack Obama faced fierce opposition when he attempted to raise the federal minimum wage above $7.25 an hour. Workers cannot sit back and entrust their lives to politicians. Whether for a request for a friendly work schedule or for income adjustment, a boycott is the ultimate way to get people out of such a crisis. Peak seasons should be targeted. No business can tolerate a whole week of inactivity during peak demand. If business owners harden their hearts, like Pharaoh before the man of God, Moses, another week or two of boycott should follow, till the workers' voices are heard. With regard to similar demands or requests elsewhere, workers can agree across the country or state to just stay home and relax to show their concern. A boycott can be carried out within a specific company. Prior to that, the workers must prepare ahead of time for the provisions they will need for those unproductive days. It should be well planned. I advocate also for peaceful demonstrations to be carried out.

Except for health care agencies where people's lives are at stake, overtime shouldn't be mandatory in any situation in the warehouse. Goods can wait a day or two before being shipped to customers. I do not advocate for same-day or two-day shipping. On the sellers' side, their only concern is the extra cash customers pay for that service. Even in health care agencies, mandatory overtime shouldn't be prolonged. People are more prone to mistakes when the body is tired. That said, staffing coordinators should be prompted to replace employees who were fired or quit in a timely manner. They should not sit back and wait for people to build up experience elsewhere to fit their requirements, while in the meantime, their employees are burning up with too much work under mandatory over-time. They should hire people and train them. In order to build experience, one needs to start somewhere. I worked in a nursing home where the staffing coordinator openly and loudly claimed that she did not care about caregiver shortage in a given shift, and she regularly refused to call substitutes to replace people who called in absent.

I believe US laws have failed to protect citizens' rights with regard to the above. I definitely view it as a form of abuse. I have personally struggled along with others under prolonged mandatory overtime; it is heartless for managers to put that much pressure on employees who are motivated solely by a promised bonus. Certainly, employees are paid time and a half for mandatory overtimes, but the stress and health consequences of overtime outweigh this meager benefit. People with odd jobs in most states, even with mandatory overtime, still have wages below the lower income boundary of the middle class. Most people working odd jobs earn less than $20,000 a year. I used to think that someone could easily get out of poverty through education. However, my personal experience has proven me wrong. The US system is molded in such a way as to keep some people forever poor. I was shocked to discover that the government, which has the ultimate role to support citizens and open multiple doors for them, is the one dragging them down into a slimy pit by providing large school loans to students who ignorantly enroll in unaccredited colleges and/or programs. Meanwhile, the government knows that the chance of finding a position with such a degree is very slim. This is another form of abuse that needs to be addressed. The government should not only care about the taxes collected from for-profit schools and universities. Poor victims are buried in debt that cannot be voided through bankruptcy filing. The ultimate solution here would be to lend only to students enrolled in both accredited schools and programs.

Another solution for the government would be to define the curriculum of each program and have all colleges and universities abide by it, to make all schools and programs accredited. Moreover, schools should emphasize the names of majors and/or concentrations in any program. All job applications I came across wanted to know one's major. My major was public health. This is so vague and meaningless. It would have been a more appealing name if it resonated like biostatistics, epidemiology, or health program planning and evaluation.

In addition, the government should enact laws compelling for-profit schools to reform their online programs in order to help students complete them or else be reimbursed. I personally was an inch away from dropping out of school because I couldn't find a practicum host. How many for-profit students drop out just because they can't find practicum sites? I met someone who was still struggling to find one after two years. Someone has to make it the responsibility of for-profit schools to place students at appropriate practicum sites. They should sign contracts for practicum purposes with many industries all over the country where they recruit students. I was told by a company that I was not eligible for a practicum because I wasn't one of their employees. I did appreciate the feedback because most places I contacted never responded to me. After searching for many weeks without success, I desperately turned to my university for help. They gave me a list of agencies to contact, which gave me a glimpse of hope. To my surprise, many of those agencies provided negative feedback, such as "Sorry, we do not do such things in our company" or "We do not meet the school's requirements." After losing all hope, a company out of the blue contacted me just a couple of days before the deadline. This felt like the hand of God. Despite the unfruitful investment, I am so grateful to God for allowing me to complete the program. What a desperate situation it is for those who, after investing that much, are still left empty-handed. I wish all previous students had the opportunity to complete their programs, and that future ones will as well. Unplanned events may certainly prevent that from happening, but preventable circumstances should not in any way shatter people's hopes and dreams.

For-profit universities providing online classes should have a practicum placement specialist in each state to ensure placement of all students in various practicum sites. Just for illustrational purposes, if such specialists were paid $60,000 a year, it would be a total expenditure of $3,000,000 yearly, assuming one representative per state plus office fees and other expenses. Somebody in this assignment could have his/her office at home. This expenditure could be directly deducted from the CEO's income, leaving the CEO with an average income of

$4,000,000, which is still a lot of money. Other board members with multimillion-dollar bonuses could chip in as well. This is not too much to ask from them. It's just a fair investment on behalf of students, who constitute the foundation on which they build their well-being. Please give them room to smile too!

Managers, especially in warehouses, use mandatory overtime for peak time crisis mitigation. But to my understanding, and from a humanitarian point of view, this creates many other problems that need to be addressed. The health risks to which employees are exposed under prolonged mandatory overtime have been presented above. Another issue that managers care less about is that a hectic schedule forces most employees out of a job. This hurts the US economy as a whole, and ex-workers become a burden on the government. When employees can't take it anymore, they quit, and employers spend much time training new workers instead of having knowledgeable employees carrying out tasks. For example, there were about twelve people when I started at Warehouse II; three days later about ten other people joined us, and by the time I quit two and a half months later, only four were left. Other people who arrived after us in small groups of two, three, and four had quit before I did. From my experience in warehouses, I learned that some folks in the United States would love to hold a full time job in a specific agency but limit themselves to seasonal work only because they cannot make a career in most industries due to the hard work environment coupled with the point system. I talked with a colleague at Warehouse II who longed, like many others, to make a career; unfortunately, the point policy kicked her out just a couple of weeks after she began because she had to babysit her grandchild on Saturdays. I frankly do not understand why employers deny a weekend off to somebody who has already accumulated overtime from Monday through Friday, for a prolonged period of time. A simple boycott can solve the problem of mandatory overtime if employees are of one accord and refuse to show up on Saturday and/or Sunday. No manager would fire all employees in one day. It would be like committing suicide. People should not let heartless managers torture and/or manipulate them like that. With one accord, people can make their voices heard.

Parents and especially mothers have a hard time balancing such work schedules with family responsibilities. They are trapped between the obligation of providing food and shelter to their offspring and unfriendly work schedules that deny them the right to care for their families. Under such pressure most parents, and especially single ones, have a tendency to neglect their kids because they must work hard to pay the multiple bills awaiting them. What I mean by neglecting kids is that, after a mandatory ten- to fourteen-hour shift, they have neither the strength nor the energy to discipline them, for example, seeing to it that homework is done well. In order to have a bit of rest at home after work, they keep kids busy with all sorts of video games, iPads, computer games, TV, movies, and others, which unfortunately puts those kids on the path to addiction. No wonder most kids coming from poor US families are set for academic failure and less likely to attend college or university compared to those whose parents hold good jobs with an easy eight-hour work schedule Monday through Friday. Such a schedule gives them room and strength to monitor their kids after work, with the opportunity to spend quality family time together on weekends. Kids are less likely to indulge in bad behavior when parents are around. Most kids from low-income families are more likely to tread where their parents have trod, finding themselves caught in a vicious circle.

Despite the multitude of workers hired by some employers at peak time, things don't always go well for them due to poor managerial skills and choices. As a consequence, they lose some temporary employees just at the time they are needed the most. Most managers earn their positions after many years of experience in the company and do not necessarily have the managerial skills taught in business schools. They hire people ahead of time to train and get them ready for peak time, which is commendable. At Warehouse II as mentioned above, by the time peak season kicked in, a lot of temp workers had already quit, and the remaining employees were already worn out from needless mandatory overtimes. Despite the stimulating bonuses offered (tens of dollars), people were not excited at all when being told that the coming weeks would be hectic. This announcement came at a time when all employees were longing for and dreaming of a break, and instead they were told that the break would have to wait a couple of weeks.

These managers obviously care little about the physical ability of employees to handle the job without break. They just want the job done, and that's it. Did slave owners care about the physical ability of their human properties in performing assignments? People are used like robots: plug in to outlets that never run out of energy. The shocking part is that because of their extremely low incomes, these mandatory overtimes cannot get poor people out of poverty; rather, they put people in a position to indulge in risky behaviors such as those mentioned above. Sending managers to business school under scholarships or hiring school-trained managers would help in this crisis. In addition, treating people with respect and dignity is also a solution that should be implemented.

With regard to the safety net service and under the present conditions of low income, the government should let people work as many hours as they want to, and then have them contribute a certain amount toward their health insurance, housing, and food. For example, instead of limiting my colleague to working thirty-nine hours in two weeks, let her work forty hours every week like she used to do, and then have her contribute, let's say, 1 percent, 2 percent, or 3 percent of every dollar earned above the thirty-nine-hour threshold toward whatever services she is receiving from the government. To my understanding, in order to be eligible for assistance, the government should require a minimum number of hours of work from nondisabled people.

Chapter 6

Another Stumbling Block for Low-Income Individuals: The So-Called Deductible in Health Insurance and Pharmaceutical Products

People with low incomes in the United States face another challenge or stumbling block from the system on the way to maintaining them as forever poor. They work hard but with no hope. They cannot lean on employers for a suitable income. Yet when dealing with health problems such as the consequences of energy drinks and others, the health care system denies them adequate services. When some health services are provided, health insurance companies refuse to pay the bills due to high deductibles. The poor find themselves trapped in a system that crushes them on all sides with no mercy or remorse. People may believe that the three entities, employers, health care providers, and health insurance companies, conspire together against them. In fact, the actual stimulus behind this is greed; it moves all of the entities independently to act the way they do, discriminating against the poor.

Before the establishment of health insurance policies, doctors knew that patients may or may not be able to pay for services they provided and would not take the chance on providing unnecessary services. With the establishment of health insurance policies, doctors became confident that they would be paid for their services. This stimulated greed in them, and they started "making decisions about the patient's care with no consideration of cost, leading to escalating medical costs and increasing numbers of uninsured citizens whose access to care is limited" (Schneider 2011, 446). Schneider stressed that hospital bills in the United States have skyrocketed more than general inflation (Schneider 2011, 459). The problem of medical costs in the United States has its roots in the cruel nature of capitalism, which includes the freedom to pursue interests even in an unethical way: freedom of pharmaceutical companies to set product prices as high as it pleases them; freedom of doctors and hospitals to set prices for their services as high as desired in order to make as much money as possible from insurance companies; freedom of doctors to increase the quantity of services even when some are useless, stimulated by the money incentive; freedom of patients to sue doctors for malpractice, even with false claims, motivated by huge rewards; freedom to pay employees $7.25/hour and CEOs multiple millions in addition to bonuses; freedom of the insurer to set deductibles to protect the company from paying hospital bills of the poor, who are bound to choose low coverage options with high deductibles due to low income.

In my opinion, nothing except greed can explain elevated health care costs in the United States. In 2001, I had a C-section in Germany and had to spend about ten days in the hospital with the baby. During those ten days, I had a CAT scan and was put on antibiotics. All the services I received (C-section, food, CAT scan, room, antibiotics) cost about 2,600 Deutschmarks, approximately $1,460. The insurance covered 90 percent of that bill. In 2004, a friend in Sweden was charged 6,000 Krona or $841.20, all-inclusive, for normal delivery in a remote hospital; the hospital in the city of Umeå had the higher price of 10,000 Krona or $1,402. As an immigrant with no social security number, she paid out of pocket because of no insurance (there is universal health coverage for all residents of Sweden with SSNs). In 2007, I had a normal delivery in Louisville, Kentucky, spent three days in the hospital, underwent a CAT scan, and received no antibiotics; my bill was a little bit over $18,000, and the baby's was around $13,000. What a gap! This is an unpleasant game, especially for the poor. I didn't notice much difference in terms of service quality among the three countries.

On March 17, 2015, I had outpatient surgery, which itself lasted fifteen minutes and took place at 1:00 p.m.;

however, I had to come in at 11:00 a.m. for paperwork, and I left the building around 2:30 p.m. For the three and half hours of service and presence in the hospital, a bill of $8,452.22 was served; my insurance negotiated $4,751.01 off the bill and further contributed an amount of $1,585.85, which left us with a total cost of $2,115.36. Prior to the surgery, the surgeon had requested a deposit of $178 in addition to the twenty-dollar copayment.

Why do US hospitals overcharge patients? Why do insurers have to negotiate fees down? Couldn't the hospitals and doctors charge the discounted fees in the first place? One reason insurers give to justify why they shouldn't pay the bill is that they bargain the price for the patient. Given the way the health care system is built in the United States, the poor won't make it unless the government demands a minimum income of at least twenty dollars per hour, so that everyone can acquire good policies with no deductible, or the government otherwise mandates bonus distributions from the least to the top employee. Health insurance policies with no deductibles are available in the United States but can be afforded only by rich people. The poor could be included in such policies if CEOs and their surrounding clans could get rid of greed.

Because of greed, the medical establishment in the United States has opposed multiple governmental attempts to help the poor or control the cost of health care services. Thank God for some battles won by the government.

For example, "early in the 20th century, they opposed the establishment of public health clinics and centers in order to protect their economic interest" (Schneider 2011, 446). Another opposition by the medical establishment was against prescriptions for kids diagnosed by school doctors or nurses (Schneider 2011, 448). Under these frustrating circumstances, school nurses and doctors had no choice but just to send a note to parents informing them of their child's health condition (Schneider 2011, 448). I wonder how those school doctors and nurses felt after repeatedly diagnosing a given child with the same health problem year after year without authorization to prescribe medications.

Another example is the vehement opposition of medical professionals against a bacteriology laboratory established by the New York Department of Health (Schneider 2011, 447). In fact, this laboratory was marketing an antitoxin drug to cure diphtheria that was produced in-house and prescribing it to poor people at no cost: "The medical profession accused the New York Department of Health of socialism and an unfair competition" (Schneider 2011, 447).

Meanwhile, they (Republicans) do not view low-income policies as unfair to those earning low incomes. They do not consider it to be unfair for the government to provide welfare services to low-income people with full-time jobs in private companies while CEOs and board members live lavishly, squandering their wealth on private jets, multimillion-dollar mansions, $100,000 pedicures, luxurious cruises, and the list goes on. At the same time, their employees, the very people sustaining the companies, get up at 2:00 a.m., 3:00 a.m., 4:00 a.m., or 5:00 a.m. regardless of the weather, for ten- to twelve-hour shifts or even more; they are on their feet, in some places with mandatory overtimes, under stimulants and/or pain pills, and yet struggling to put food on their tables with no suitable health care coverage.

The medical profession cannot perceive it as unfair because of greed. I remember, during my prenatal visits in a family health center in 2007, I overheard a medical doctor bragging about a $300,000 cruise she had just taken. She had just returned to work after that lavish trip. It wasn't fun at all for me to hear. I was getting my prenatal visit there, like many others, due to lack of insurance. After delivery, I received a bill from the hospital of more than $13,000 for the baby and $18,000 for myself. Thank God, the government took care of these. How many US citizens file for bankruptcy because of hospital bills? Low-income people spend their lives gathering crumbs from under the tables of investors, CEOs, and board members. Health industries seize the opportunity of illness to squeeze the poor of their crumbs, leaving them buried in debt, in order to allow to a few splendor and lavish lives, while health insurance companies hide behind deductibles to deny help. It is only in a capitalist system that workers purchase health insurance policies and still pay hospital bills out of pocket because of greed.

According to the Census Bureau, 37.1 percent of employed American workers live below the poverty level (Census Bureau 2014a). These are people who, despite hard work, still rely on safety net programs to survive. Another group of unfortunate workers are those whose income put them slightly above the poverty line as defined by the Census Bureau; they are still poor but not poor enough to qualify for safety net programs. I worked with a single mom at Warehouse III during peak time in 2015, who told me how difficult it was for her to find a babysitter. She couldn't afford daycare due to her low income. However, that meager income was large enough to disqualify her from childcare assistance. It is absurd that the government provides welfare to private companies' workers in order for them to make it through, while bosses earn multiple millions of dollars coupled with bonuses.

Chapter 7

The Cost of Medical Services: A Stumbling Block for Low-Income Individuals

As mentioned above, many low-income workers in the United States have trouble accessing medical care when needed because they cannot afford health insurance. Some parents may be offered minimal insurance policies from employers, while their offspring remain uninsured because family plans are unaffordable. The shocking thing is that individuals with low-quality insurance but no serious illness pay most or all of their hospital bills out-of-pocket because of deductibles. It has been proven that the difficulty in accessing medical services for low-income individuals stems from high costs (Schneider 2011, 461). Due to escalating hospital bills, insurers have increased monthly premiums, with employers increasingly shifting the burden to their workers (Schneider 2011, 461) who, for the most part, are already struggling under low incomes. Schneider argued that under this crisis, employers have sat back, making employees contribute "a larger share of premiums, higher deductibles, and higher copayments" (Schneider 2011, 461). Given high premiums, some low-income employees definitely waive insurance plans (Schneider 2011, 461), but are not qualified for Medicaid because their wages put them slightly above the poverty line (Schneider 2011, 461). Meanwhile, uninsured individuals in general tend to procrastinate receiving medical (or a similar verb) services when they feel sick (Schneider 2011,462).

Once, we unknowingly took our child to the adult emergency room at University of Louisville Hospital. While we were still in the waiting room, a nurse approached us and warned us not to get the child registered, adding that they did not have the proper equipment for kids and advising us to take the child to Kosair Norton Hospital instead. She stressed that if the child's name entered the system, even without receiving any service, we might still have a bill of three thousand dollars. Why? Emergency rooms in the United States seem to be the place for uninsured hardworking individuals and others to go when in need of medical care. In general, such individuals seek medical care at the emergency room when they can't procrastinate anymore. Indeed, it is a violation of law for emergency rooms to deny care to the poor and uninsured in some states (Schneider 2011, 445). However, after the emergency crisis is handled, hospitals in some states send uninsured patients away, and they may seek care in charity or public health centers (Schneider 2011, 445). Uninsured individuals are more likely to die from preventable diseases and/or develop chronic diseases because they tend to postpone hospital visits when they feel sick.

The Medicare program is on the verge of bankruptcy. Due to the rising cost of medical services, the programs disburse more money than they collect in premiums (Schneider 2011, 462). One may think that the expensive health care in the United States comes with outstanding results. Instead, it is known that US citizens have poorer health than citizens in other developed countries (Schneider 2011, 463), and especially where health care is free for all. She stressed that "an international comparison of thirty-seven countries in 2005 indicated that the United States ranked thirtieth in infant mortality and twenty-third and twenty-fifth for life expectancy in males and females, respectively, in 2004" (Schneider 2011, 460).

Chapter 8

The Reasons behind the Rising Costs of Hospital Bills in the United States

Let me go back to my experience at University of Louisville in 2007 when giving birth to our fourth kid. I went to the emergency room due to lack of insurance. This is something we ought to be grateful for. Otherwise the poor in the United States could be in the position of giving birth in their bedrooms. Following their routine, they measured my blood pressure, temperature, and weight and requested a urine sample, which I provided. The next step was the delivery room, on the third floor. To my great surprise, the nurses there handed me a container for a urine specimen.

I said, "Hold on. That has been taken care of just about thirty minutes ago on the first floor, and they can send you the results."

She said I was in a different department, and what they did was independent from what the other department had done. I had my blood pressure, temperature, and weight remeasured. With such an unorganized system, customers might be billed two, three, or more times for the same service, while data could just travel from one department to the other in the computer age; this would save sick people, especially those with a low income, a lot of money. It was about 11:00 a.m. that day when the doctor in charge checked my cervix for the first time; after a second check at noon, I was told that I was four centimeters dilated. A few minutes after she left, I was in deep pain and remembered the pills that Swedes give women in labor to ease pain throughout the process. I said to myself, "Maybe similar pills are also here, and I just need to ask." The nurse responded they did not have such pills. After a few minutes, I thought about an epidural. In Sweden, when those pills don't work, women are immediately administered an epidural. So I went back to the nurse and pleaded for that. Unfortunately, I got a very disturbing answer.

"You are asking for pain pills when the doctor wants to send you home. She will come back at 1:00 p.m., and if you are still four centimeters dilated, she will send you home," she replied.

I went back dejected, suspecting that this was because I had no health insurance. Thank God, when she came back at 1:00 p.m., I was eight centimeters

dilated. By the way she shouted out loudly, "Eight centimeters dilated!" I could tell she was greatly surprised.
That was my miracle. What would have happened to me
and the baby if I had walked out of that hospital at four
centimeters dilated? Let's assume that at 1:00 p.m. I
was sent home only to come back later that day. I would
have had to go through for a second time the whole reg-
istration process and undergo all the exams and tests
I had undergone in the morning on both the first and
third floors.

Another issue behind the rising cost of health care is the
huge amount of paperwork it involves. I do not understand how the most developed country on the planet fails
in that. In Sweden, for example, each individual with a
lawful residence of one year or more is provided a social
security number. At the hospital, this number is used by
the nurse or doctor to access all of one's health-related
information. At the immigration offices, that same number provides all information concerning one's immigration status. In the United States, the first visit at a medical
office or service is decorated by paperwork, and a lot of
it. Although there is nothing wrong with that per se, one
has to provide the same personal information such as
first name, last name, address, social security number,
and phone number on each form, even if ten of them are
served. In addition, personal information is requested at
each visit.

Another key reason highlighted by Schneider (2011) for rising health care costs is the "fee-for-service system of payment, which gives medical providers a lot of financial incentives" (Schneider 2011, 464). With this system in place, the more services provided, the more money doctors make. Therefore, doctors, out of greed, increase service numbers with the sole purpose to augment their income (Schneider 2011, 464). This game suffocates the low income with unpleasant bills. For example, I took one of our daughters to the emergency room. She had had a splinter in her foot for two weeks. Despite antibiotic treatment, pus continued to come out. After an X-ray exam in the emergency room, we waited about four to five hours for the doctor to declare that the X-ray revealed nothing, and that she was requesting an ultrasound for further assessment. I suspected the ultrasound was ordered just to increase the bill. After another long hour of waiting, they finally came and got the splinter out. It had been about 6:00 p.m. when we got there, and we left only after midnight. I later learned that the more one stays in the ER, the more money is requested in terms of bills. Why torture people like that to squeeze off their crumbs? We were kept there for about seven hours to receive a thirty- to forty-five-minute service. Medical doctors should have fixed salaries in order to stop such awful acts.

Schneider asserted that doctors earn more money for surgical procedures using high-tech diagnostic instruments than they do relying on symptoms in the diagnostic process (Schneider 2011, 464). No wonder more women in the United States give birth by C-section than by normal delivery. A colleague of mine once joked that when the baby's head is already showing up, they push the little one back in the womb in order to rush you to the surgical room. A study conducted in four hospitals in the United States revealed that 81.2 percent of caesarean sections done in those hospitals were not justified (Lauer and Lauer 2011, 389). Schneider pointed out that in the American medical market, doctors are the ones who set prices for their services, while the insurance companies are responsible for paying the bill (Schneider 2011, 464); as a consequence, doctors are guaranteed that they will be paid for their services and care less about selecting the least expensive method of treatment. The more expensive the options used in providing care, the higher the doctors' incomes. Why should they then care?

Another method doctors use to increase bills is to shoulder each other with unnecessary referrals. For example, during the routine doctor's visit in my fifth pregnancy, I was diagnosed with low iron levels; instead of prescribing me iron pills, my doctor referred me to a blood disorder disease doctor because they have a most expensive and fancy way to administer iron through injections or by IV. Because of that, I had to be followed by two doctors throughout that pregnancy. Glory to God, the blood disorder disease doctor put me first on iron pills. This eventually worked for me. She did explain that some people do not tolerate those pills, but did my first doctor even try them? No. Thumbs-up to the blood doctor and to anyone in that field that does not mistake patients for an ATM machine.

Finally, medical school tuition in the United States is another key factor explaining the extremely high health-care bills. Medical students find themselves buried in debt upon completion of their training. I have heard medical students speak of owing $500,000 in school loans. Munro stated that median loans contracted by medical students in a four-year course of training are $278,445 and $207,868 at private and public schools, respectively, with living costs included (Munro, 2014). Most of these loans are unsubsidized and accrue interest right away. After graduation, most physicians seek another loan for expensive cars and new houses to match their new status. This being said, a medical doctor in the United States may start his/her career with about a million dollars of debt. The obvious question is this: "Who will pay those bills?" The simple answer is that individuals seeking medical care will indirectly be responsible. Let's remember that some of those seeking healthcare services earn $7.25, $8.00, or $15.00 an hour. Large numbers of US workers fall into this income category. This issue needs to be addressed.

In other developed countries (e.g., Germany), medical school entrance is based solely on selection. The government selects the best students graduating from high school, and they attend medical school tuition-free.

By comparison, a high income constitutes one of the most common motivations for becoming a physician in the United States. Few are the US folks attending medical school out of love for the field. Thumbs-up for those who get in out of love! Some medical school aspirants do not even worry about getting a huge loan because they plan to ransom patients, including the poor, to pay off the debt. I once heard of another medical student whose parents paid off his tuition, rent, and nutrition out of their own pockets. Yet he still managed to borrow up to $250,000 to squander in fun activities as a student. Why should someone do that? Maybe because such a fellow plans to transfer the debt burden to those who seek medical services. That is likely why patients are overcharged.

Chapter 9

Failed Attempts at Cost Control

Giving the persistent problem of high medical costs, the government and some employers have attempted to reduce the burden but without success. Schneider argued that the first attempt to control medical costs was conducted by President Nixon between 1971 and 1974 (Schneider 2011, 465). His approach aimed at enforcing a price control, which helped slow down the cost increase, but just for a short period of time (Schneider 2011, 465). To counterattack that policy, doctors multiplied the amount of services provided to patients, to make up for the loss (Schneider 2011, 465). Consequently, Nixon's policy died quickly, and medical costs kept rising (Schneider 2011, 465). The second attempt, implemented in the 1970s, aimed at cutting spending on new medical facilities and supplies (Schneider 2011, 465). A regional planning agency was put in place by the federal government with the mission to assess the need for new materials in medical centers and issue a certificate of need, which was used for purchasing the required materials (Schneider 2011, 465). Unfortunately, the regional planning agency failed to carry out that assignment, and the project collapsed in the 1980s (Schneider 2011, 465). The third attempt to control medical costs was implemented in the 1980s, surely after the above failure, but it had a short life-span like the earlier ones. This time the government attempted to decrease hospital stays for inpatients under Medicare by contributing a flat fee toward hospital bills regardless of the hospitalization duration (Schneider 2011, 465). Under this policy medical facilities had the choice between shortening the hospital stay and keeping the extra cash or voiding the additional costs that come with prolonged stays (Schneider 2011, 465). As a result the length of a hospital stay effectively declined. To overturn this, hospitals targeted private insurance industries and began charging them more for the same services (Schneider 2011, 465). In addition, doctors turned most patients into outpatients and provided care out of the government's sight, with medical costs continuing to rise (Schneider 2011, 465). Physicians discharging patients under this policy suggests that prior to it, some inpatients could well be treated as outpatients, relieving their financial burden. In contrast to the American system, German hospitals send any patient away when the medical condition does not require hospitalization. They have no incentive in doing so because physicians are on salaries and, as mentioned above, got their training for free. Inpatient care is solely reserved for hospitals, and outpatient facilities are mainly small clinics. This way the patient is not billed for needless services.

Employers and insurance companies challenged the rising of hospital costs by establishing what they called managed care in the 1990s. Under this policy, insurance companies sign contracts with a couple of selected doctors who agree to provide care to their patients at an affordable cost (Schneider 2011, 466). The trick in this policy is that the patient must know the list of doctors selected by his/her insurance company. If, out of ignorance, the patient goes to a doctor not selected by the insurance company, the insurer will refuse to pay the bill. Many US patients have been trapped this way, finding themselves stuck with thousands of dollars in hospital bills unpaid by the insurer. Another health insurance plan under managed care allows the patient to seek care by nonselected doctors, with the obligation to pay most of the bills out of pocket (Schneider 2011, 466). Another form of managed care instituted in the 1990s is the health maintenance organization (HMO), which operates as an insurer and provider simultaneously (Schneider 2011, 466). This organization hires its own medical professionals and puts them on salaries (Schneider 2011, 466). As a result, they are not under the temptation of providing expensive nonrequired treatments (Schneider 2011, 466). On the contrary, they benefit more in providing preventive services to patients in order to avoid chronic diseases that would cost a lot in the long run (Schneider 2011, 466).

Given the outstanding results in reducing hospital bills in the managed care plan, employers encouraged their employees to enroll in that program. As of 1995, about three-quarters of employees insured through their companies were enrolled in managed care (Schneider 2011, 466). Even the government started enrolling individuals under Medicaid into that program as a means to control the cost (Schneider 2011, 467). Unfortunately, like other plans mentioned above, the life-span of managed care was very short. Patients quickly denounced the practice of denying some services as inappropriate (Schneider 2011, 466). Even though they couldn't prove whether the denied services were necessary or not, such complaints led to the downfall of managed care (Schneider 2011, 467). However, some complaints were appropriate. For example, managed care, motivated by money incentives, put into place drive-through services such as mastectomies coupled with the shortening of hospital stays of some patients who underwent major surgery (Schneider 2011, 467). Even though managed care has not completely disappeared, it has lost its outreach and strength, giving way to the escalating cost of medical care experienced today (Schneider 2011, 467).

The last attempt at controlling health care costs was set up during the Bush presidency and referred to as a consumer-directed health plan (CDHP) (Schneider 2011, 467). I personally do not comprehend how this plan could have positive effects in controlling hospital bills. Solving a problem requires one to go to its root, identifying the issue and then finding a solution. Scratching the surface while ignoring its roots was merely a waste of time. This plan aimed at raising patient awareness of healthcare costs, inviting them to bear more of the expenses (Schneider 2011, 467). Right! This plan protects insurers and prevents them from paying bills unless the customer pays the deductible (Schneider 2011, 467). The deductible, decided solely by the insurer, is so high that most people with low incomes cannot in any way afford it. Someone earning $15,000, $20,000, or $25,000 a year cannot afford a deductible of $10,000, $7,000, or $5,000 for receiving perhaps a week of hospital service. The imbalance is ridiculous and cannot work.

Let's consider an individual earning $20,000 a year with an insurance policy requiring a $5,000 deductible per year. Let's assume that this person has three short visits at the hospital throughout the year for minor issues and was charged $1,000, $1,500, and $2,500 for them, respectively. Because these bills equal the deductible in total, the insurer would contribute nothing toward them. The individual certainly has health insurance but is still paying bills out of pocket. This is nothing short of abuse. Let's assume that the bills totaled $5,001. The insurer's contribution would be a dollar for that year. This is outrageous.

Even if the patient opens a tax-free savings account as this last plan requires, it still does not sound right that someone pays a monthly premium toward health insurance and does not benefit from it. Moreover, when basic needs are not met, it is unlikely that someone will set up a savings account, whether taxed or not. Another funny thing is that the contribution toward the deductible in one year is not taken into account for the next year. It is, however, important to mention that some insurers paid routine or check-up visits at 100 percent as long as no diseases have been diagnosed.

A final observation is that US pharmaceutical products are much cheaper abroad than they are in the United States. Drugs are generally unaffordable by low income folks in the most developed country on earth. Fortunately, generic drugs can help. Reinhardt (2009) asserts that the fact that "the prices of patented drugs can be so much lower abroad than is charged, on average, for the same drugs in the United States has long irritated American politicians and the general public" (Reinhardt 2009). In response to this crisis, a bipartisan team in Congress attempted without success to amend the Senate health care reform bill to allow American pharmacies and patients to import prescription drugs from other countries, like Canada, at lower, government-controlled prices, including drugs developed and manufactured in the United States and exported to these countries (Reinhardt 2009).

If Congress had succeeded with the above amendment to the healthcare reform bill, not only would American drugs be imported, but the door would be largely open to foreign pharmaceutical companies, which would invade the US drug market with cheap and affordable products. The US drug market would be competitive enough to force US pharmaceutical companies to reduce prices, rendering drugs affordable for low-income people.

Chapter 10

Low-Income and Poor Work Schedules Can Promote Abortion

Why do people kill their unborn children? Among other reasons is poverty. Republicans shout out loud on every media that they are pro-life. Agree! Yet they refuse to raise a finger to help the parents in need. Why do they sabotage all efforts to increase the minimum wage? They like to quote the scripture saying that "whoever does not work should not eat" (2 Thess. 3:10). Great! They rely on this scripture to speak evil about social services and hinder them by all means. Why not pay well those who strive and toil hard in their industries in order to get them off of government welfare? In the Bible it is also written, "So give to the needy what you greedily possess and you will be clean all over" (Luke 11:41). Abortion is a stumbling block for Democrats who endorse the implantation of abortion clinics.

I have heard many people say that they cannot afford to have another child in daycare. It is too expensive for low-income and middle-class workers. What would a low-income single mom do if she finds herself pregnant again? Despite the hardship of raising kids in the United States, some women in such circumstances would choose to keep the child, while others would go straight to an abortion clinic. Moms with one or more kids in the United States are more likely to lose their jobs. The system has indeed done little to discourage abortion. When employers request mandatory overtime as I experienced in Warehouse II, they care less about moms. A colleague in a nursing home once told me that in order to get to work at 7:00 a.m. as scheduled, she had to get up at around 5:00 a.m. to get her two kids ready for daycare. In a situation like the one at Warehouse II, where the starting time was moved from 7:00 a.m. to 5:00 a.m. from time to time, this mom would have to get her kids up at 3:00 a.m. to prepare them for daycare. Why should little innocent kids go through that? Can they not give parents in general a special treatment? For example, they could allow them to keep regular schedules even during peak times. In the long run, such a pace will be very stressful for parents and kids as well. When parents, and especially single moms, cannot find a good balance between work and family, they cannot push their kids off the cliff; most of them quit their jobs and apply for safety net programs. When the mother knows well the maternity bills and difficulties she would go through after birth, choosing abortion could be an easy pick. However, in the case of an unplanned pregnancy, a good income and work schedule could prevent the thought of abortion.

Abortion Statistics

I strongly believe that abortion is a significant public health problem that needs to be addressed. According to the Guttmacher Institute (2013), a staggering number of 54,559,615 abortions took place in the United States between 1973 and 2008. Women with a history of abortion include 18 percent of teenagers aged fifteen to seventeen (Guttmacher Institute 2013). More than 50 percent of all cases are recorded among women in their twenties, while 33 percent and 24 percent are among women aged twenty to twenty-four and twenty-five to twenty-nine, respectively (Guttmacher Institute 2013). When classified by race, current statistics show that 36 percent of women with a history of abortion are non-Hispanic white, while 30 percent and 25 percent are black or African American and Hispanic women, respectively (Guttmacher Institute 2013). Looking into religious categories, the Guttmacher Institute (2013) found that 37 percent of women who aborted during the study time frame were Protestants, while 28 percent were Catholics. Single women who have never engaged in a marital relationship accounted for 45 percent of all abortion cases registered (Guttmacher Institute 2013). Women who were already moms with one or more kids accounted for

61 percent of all abortion cases (Guttmacher Institute 2013). Interestingly, 42 percent of those women acknowledged having an income below the federal poverty level (Guttmacher Institute 2013).

Another research study conducted by the Guttmacher Institute on nonhospital patients across the United States indicated that people who aborted in 2014 were largely poor and low-income (Guttmacher Institute 2016). Of all those who aborted, 75 percent were poor or had low incomes; 49 percent had an income below 100 percent of the federal poverty level, while 29 percent were among the low-income population with an income between 100 percent to 199 percent of the federal poverty level (Guttmacher Institute 2016). For clarification purposes only, if the government sets the poverty level at $20,000 a year for a household of three, it would be said for a household of that size earning $39,800 that they are at 199 percent of poverty level. That is 1.99 $20,000= $39,800. Or if that family has an income of $10,000 a year instead, they will be at 50 percent below poverty level.

Other Reasons for Abortion

Women who abort provide different reasons to justify their actions, some of which were highlighted by Torres and Forrest (1988). Some women who participated in their study revealed that they opted for abortion because the coming baby would bring changes in their routine lives; others thought they were not ready to have a baby due to the responsibility that comes with it. Still others wanted to avoid being single moms due to unstable relationships with the prospective fathers of their coming babies (Torres and Forrest, 1988). Alternatively, some were trying to hide their pregnancy, probably from parents or relatives; others were thought to be too young to have a child (Torres and Forrest 1988). In addition, some women claimed they were already moms and did not want more kids; in some cases, the partner or parents requested abortion (Torres and Forrest 1988). Other reasons included the fetus or mom having health problems and/or conception occurring as a result of rape or incest (Torres and Forrest 1988).

In all cases, the abortive action leads to loss of life and a violation of the right to be born for those poor babies. The consequences can be traced both to the personal and economic levels. At the economic level, the slaughtering of babies constitutes a huge workforce that is lost. To fill the gap, the United States has put into place migration policies to attract highly skilled workers from other countries. At the personal level, it is proven that women who have aborted face a great deal of emotional problems. The American Pregnancy Association claimed that the emotional and psychological problems women go through after abortion include regret, depression, anger, feelings of guilt, loneliness or isolation, shame, loss of self-confidence, insomnia or nightmares, relationship issues, suicidal thoughts and feelings, eating disorders, and anxiety (American Pregnancy Association 2013). This report stressed that emotional problems after abortion vary from one woman to another depending on many factors, such as religious beliefs that oppose abortion, a person being forced or persuaded to abort, and a person with previous emotional issues (American Pregnancy Association 2013).

New Policies to Address Abortion

The ultimate solution to abortion is to enact a law that bans it for good, tear down abortion clinics all over the country, and impose fines on or prosecute anybody who violates that law. Other methods consist of encouraging abstinence before marriage and improving the economic situation of women by enacting laws that:

* Provide decent income to everybody so that they may be able to pay for daycare if needed.
* Encourage big companies to provide daycare services to employees, and have employees contribute a monthly fee depending on their income level.
* Put into place paid leave for moms as advocated by Ivanka Trump by requiring employers to keep on paying moms when they are on maternity leave. If not, the government should step in and pay lost wages due to childbirth. The governments in some developed countries give moms and/or dads up to 80 percent of their income during that period of transition.
* Assure moms that they will have their positions back after maternity leave.

* Give moms six months to a year of maternity leave in order to give them a chance to invest time in the lives of their little ones, as is done in other developed countries like Sweden, Canada, and Germany.

In Sweden, for example, the government encourages parents via child and parent allowances to stay home with the newborn baby. This removes the financial burden that comes with the birth of a new child. According to Swedish law, a maximum of 480 parental days are granted to parents with a newborn baby, among which 390 are quite well-paid days in case the parent held a job prior to the coming of the newborn. When the baby is still under the age of one, both working parents can stay home to care for the baby full-time, even if the allowance is not requested at a full-time rate. When the baby turns one, a parent may still stay home at a full-time rate but runs the risk of declined levels of other social benefits. Therefore, such a parent is required to use at least five of the seven weekdays in order to avoid the cutdown on the level of some social benefits. The Swedish government grants free health care to all children and makes it cheap and affordable to adults.

In addition, every visit to the midwife is free of charge for all pregnant women. Even though abortion remains an option there, the system has made everything easy for parents, and especially women, to shun abortion. The

Swedish people are not scared of the burden of having a child like the case in the most powerful country in the world. Interestingly enough, the Swedish government encourages the birth of a second child within a two-and-a-half-year frame by putting well-paid days at the same level for the second baby as well. The Swedish government retains part of the allowances and invests them automatically into the parents' retirement plan. This is amazing because it gives the possibility to unemployed parents to have a retirement plan as well.

By contrast, US pro-life advocates do not lift a finger to ease things on parents, and women especially. To the contrary, any endeavor to help kids and parents is labeled as socialism. They spend time coloring in red the black side of socialism, which in reality shouldn't be encouraged by any means; meanwhile, they color in white the black side of capitalism because it propels them financially above the poor and the needy. Republicans have brainwashed American citizens to the point where they are nearly scared of the word socialism, not knowing that food stamps, housing allowances for single moms, Medicare, and Medicaid are, in essence, practical applications of socialism. This just needs to be extended to other areas—for example, parent and child allowances as mentioned above; daycare subsidies; free healthcare, at least for all kids, like in Sweden; free tuition in public universities as advocated by Bernie Sanders. It should be remembered that the above countries have also put into place a capitalistic system that stimulates free invest-ment. However, their governments regulate some aspects of society in order to avoid all sorts of abuse such as that commonly found in the United States. I am not advocat-ing for total control by the government in every domain. However, no control from the government at all is as dangerous as absolute control. Either one comes with all sorts of abuse. To be more specific, Republicans do well in cheering and preserving moral values through con-servatism and Christianity, while Democrats do well in defending the poor and needy. Both parties should work toward a common ground.

Germany also has an outstanding social system coupled with capitalism. A working mom in Germany is entitled to maternity leave as long as she desires. There is no limit for that. However, she loses her income privilege if she has not returned to work after about three and a half years. Nevertheless, the employer must give her job back if she decides one day to go back to work. By contrast, US women are granted only three months of maternity leave, during which they remain without income, unless they have a paid time off (PTO) plan. For some, the paid time off fund runs out within a week or two if they have not worked long enough to accrue substantial money. This is when such individuals need money the most, to provide for the newborn kids, but no one reaches out to help: there is no child allowance or parent allowance.

Some women shorten their maternity leave because of financial distress. What a shame for the most powerful country on earth! Americans refuse to invest in the very ones who will uphold their future economy, running the risk of seeing everything collapse.

In this imperfect world, the policies mentioned above cannot stop abortion completely but would help save thousands of lives each year. They would prevent moms/women from being apprehensive about the idea of having a child and provide assurance that their jobs will be available whenever they want to resume work; in addition, they won't have to worry about bills during maternity leave, and affordable day care services would be available at work or elsewhere. I am sure that women would celebrate such policies if implemented in the United States. In a normal society, an abortion ban shouldn't be an issue. People fighting such a ban may claim that women have the right to do whatever they want with their bodies. However, the abortion issue shouldn't be about women's bodies but about the vulnerable ones whose lives are taken away: their right to be born and live is violated. Women through the ages have aborted someone that could have been the president of the United States of America, or elsewhere, an outstanding surgeon, a great preacher of all time, a great lawyer, a great lecturer, or an inventor. If somebody thinks of having fun in this life, why would you deny that pleasure to somebody that could have been your offspring, your blessings? What if you were aborted yourself?

I give a special thanks to all moms through the ages who have chosen to love and raise their kids regardless of all circumstances, whether under the sun or the rain, whether in harsh winter or scorching summer, whether with jobs or jobless, whether with husbands or single. Thumbs-up for your dedication and sacrifices. May God bless you all.

Chapter 11

The Hospital Billing System

The hospital billing system in the United States is very controversial and difficult to comprehend. It is very confusing for a patient to visit Hospital A and be billed by Hospital B. I recall a visit at Kosair Norton Hospital when our child had a splinter in her foot (see chapter 8). To our great surprise, after paying one of those bills through Kosair, University of Louisville Hospital sent us the same bill with identical codes and dollar amounts. We called University of Louisville, and, after apologizing, they told us that the doctor who provided care works for both hospitals. Was this just a mistake, or were they trying to collect money twice for the same service? We could ignore the bill already paid by us. Meanwhile, they would send it to collection agencies in order to damage our credit records.

On December 2016, I gave birth to our fifth baby at Baptist East Hospital. Due to some health problems after birth, I was hospitalized for five days. The first four days, the newborn baby underwent the same routine check and was found in perfect health, according to the attending pediatrician who repeatedly said, "The baby is fine; nothing abnormal was found." On my last hospitalization day, which happened to be a Saturday, another doctor was in charge and gave a complete different diagnosis.

"I hear a murmur in her heart," she told us, adding that she would perform a transthoracic echocardiogram test and send the results to University of Louisville or Norton Hospital for interpretation.

We agreed. Could a parent or patient say no to such a request? "Why did the results needed to be interpreted elsewhere?" I asked myself. Why for four days did the initial pediatrician miss that murmur?

After the results came back, she told us there was a hole in the baby's heart that would close up as she grew; otherwise, she may need to undergo some health intervention in the future. With this new diagnosis, an urgent follow-up was requested. From a normal healthy child, our baby was discharged with congenital heart disease. We were given a health summary to be brought to the family pediatrician at the initial routine visit the following week. The family pediatrician checked the baby, without knowing the hospital summary, and concluded that the baby was normal and healthy. Toward the end of the visit, I brought up the heart problem mentioned at the hospital. I had unfortunately forgotten to bring the hospital summary. With trained or corrupted (your choice) ears, he rechecked the baby and spoke of hearing some murmur. A follow-up with the cardiologist took place when the baby was about three months old. I was not in a rush anymore after getting two good diagnoses out of three. It came out good; the baby's heart was doing fine. In fact, the cardiologist explained that many babies are born with such a hole in the heart; for some it closes up as they grow, and for others it doesn't close up completely but does not impact the life of that person.

Throughout pregnancy I had ultrasounds at each visit, and all the results were normal. Was this doctor trying to "build up" unnecessary bills? Whether purposefully or not, her poor diagnosis of the heart murmur did add to my bill with avoidable tests and follow-ups. I was stunned when multiple bills flooded our mailbox. Among them, four were from the same source, different from Baptist East Hospital, with a request to pay at uoflphysicians. com. Two of those bills were issued on the same day in January, and the other two were also issued on the same day in February. The first (January 17, 2017) had a statement balance of $462, with the following description: previous balance of $462, with no indication of the date of service or invoice number, and the column reserved for insurance was left blank. We thought it could be related to the interpretation of the heart test conducted at Baptist

East. However, why was it described as a previous balance? What previous balance were they talking about? Our baby was just a couple of weeks old and had never been brought to University of Louisville for care.

Another bill issued on February 14, 2017, came with a statement balance of $366.91. This bill indicated a previous balance of $462 with an adjustment to the previous balance of $-462, thereby canceling the above bill. In addition, it listed the three heart tests conducted at Baptist East the day of discharge, with the date of service as well as the insurance contribution.

The second bill issued in January carried a statement balance of $1,748, also with no indication of insurance contribution. However, it indicated the date of service and the type of service, including attendance at delivery charged in the amount of $578. What does attendance at delivery mean? I recalled that around delivery time, a group of about seven women walked into the room, cheered me up during the last minutes of labor, and applauded when the baby was born. This was awesome. If these University of Louisville employees picking shifts at Baptist East charged $578 for cheering, something is wrong with that picture. I utterly disagree with that. They must be paid for their time, of course. Ten or twenty dollars should have sufficed for attending at a delivery.

The second bill issued on February 14, 2017, had a statement balance of $170.66 with statement date and type of service, as well as insurance contribution. More importantly, it carried a previous balance of $1,748 and an adjustment to the previous balance of $-1,748, thereby canceling the second bill issued in January. Each of these bills stated that insurance was pending, indicating that they were not yet settled with the insurance company. However, each came with a note stating that the amounts shown on the bill were my responsibility and a stern request to promptly pay. Of all these bills, only the one with a statement balance of $366.91 was finally listed in the health insurance online account. If I had had enough cash available, I would have sent payments upon the arrival of these bills.

Another thing that puzzled me in this billing system was being charged twice by two different companies for the same service at different rates. For example, while University of Louisville Physicians charged $462 for three heart tests, Baptist East wrapped those three exams into a cardiology-general classification and charged a colossal amount of $3,681.80. Baptist East would likely argue that University of Louisville physicians used their equipment for testing. True! Why more than $3,000? The hospital could pay University of Louisville physicians from the extra-large sums collected from patients. On what terms do hospitals hire part-time physicians? Do these physicians obtain some form of income or salary from their employers? If so, why do they send additional bills to patients? Why can't other part-time employees working for the hospital bill patients for services rendered?

Are physicians so special? After all, if part-time caregivers or nurses don't show up, a physician's work would be jeopardized. In fact, I have heard of physicians earning $250 or more per hour. If they get that much money for their labors per hour, why send an extra bill to patients at all?

Prior to understanding that some doctors bill patients separately from the hospital visited, I expected all my bills to be listed in the MyChart account under Baptist East Hospital. About two months after discharge, I received a letter from a collection company demanding payment of four bills, including the ones mentioned above. I called the billing office for an explanation.

"Why did you send my bills to a collection company?" I asked, before adding, "I have already set up a monthly payment plan with the hospital, and you will get paid at some point."

"These are doctors' bills and have nothing to do with the hospital," they replied.

Then I said, "The services I received were listed in MyChart with the names of the doctors that provided care. Who are these other doctors?"

"These are University of Louisville physicians and must bill you separately," the person told me.

"What did they do?" I asked.

"They did not have to provide any direct care. They just needed to hang around or be in the office at the time you received care. They might have done some paperwork," I heard, to my astonishment.

I do not remember receiving two of the bills that were sent to collection agencies. Regardless, I disagree with the amounts charged in the first place and those collected from patients. I strongly believe, based on my experience abroad, that insurance payment toward hospital bills are more than enough. That's probably why hospitals and doctors sell unpaid bills to collection agencies for a return of as low as 5 percent of what they claim. In their report of January 2013, the Federal Trade Commission stressed that debt collectors on average pay 4.9 cents per dollar for hospital bills (Federal Trade Commission 2013). This is another stumbling block for the middle class and the poor under the sun in the US territory. Once an unpaid bill is sent to a collection agency, the credit score of the responsible party is damaged for seven years, which precludes them from obtaining a low interest rate loan or any loan at all. Most purchases must be made in those lean years by cash only. Major purchases, such as a home, are nearly impossible. Due to low income, a person under such a crisis cannot gather enough cash for some services or borrow money due to a poor credit score. Lives are therefore turned upside down for seven years while the people responsible for it live in two-million-dollar condos and book three-hundred-thousand-dollar cruises, and the list goes on. There is nothing fair in this picture. It would have been even better if the credit damage was waived as soon as the patient paid the bills. Unfortunately, this is not the case. The Consumer Protection Financial Bureau, in its article "Consumer Experiences with Debt Collection," stressed that hospital bills are the most common debts sent to collection agencies. Among all bills collection agencies receive, about 59 percent are hospital bills (Consumer Protection Financial Bureau 2017).

Health care centers overbill their customers. Because of the free market at the root of capitalism, health care institutions and doctors are the entities deciding how much money to charge customers for specific services provided. In addition, they escalate prices to nurture their greed. Hospital bills are abnormally high and should be addressed. I have also noticed that bills from small health clinics that are hospital-owned carry hospital fees with a statement that the money collected will be shared between the hospital and physicians. This is wrong in my opinion and even outrageous. Why should hospitals charge for services provided somewhere else? Schulte, in a publication entitled "Hospital 'Facility Fees' Boosting Medical Bills, and Not Just for Hospital Care," highlighted the case of a family who routinely paid around $120 for services received at a specific health clinic (Schulte 2012). After that clinic was bought by a local hospital, the bills escalated to $1,000 for the same services (Schulte 2012). Schulte described also the case of a lady in Iowa who was billed $25,872 in facility fees for an outpatient surgery that lasted about forty-five minutes. Schulte argued that patients can also be charged large amounts of facility fees when they "seek care from private physicians that have sold their medical practices to hospitals and stay on as employees" (Schulte 2012). To justify their actions, hospitals claim that the fees collected from doctors' offices and health clinics help maintain expensive equipment, pay employees, and more importantly, cover the bills of patients who unfortunately are unable to pay (Schulte 2012).

Truth be told, this billing practice helps hospitals generate multiple billions of dollars yearly in profit. Schulte stressed that the attempt to impose the same payment rate to seniors on Medicare, regardless of whether they receive care from doctors operating independently or those employed by hospitals, failed in 2012 because five giant hospital groups opposed it, shouldered by powerful politicians on Capitol Hill (Schulte 2012). In 2012, these five hospital groups donated about "$22 million in political contributions and lobbying costs" (Schulte 2012). Such cash certainly came from overflow. Therefore, the notion that lowering fees would spell loss for their investments is a pure lie. If the $22 million was deducted from net income through hospital cost reduction instead of putting it in the hands of a couple of politicians, health care would be more affordable to virtually everybody. Mathematically speaking, it is more complicated than one would think, and my above statement might be too simplistic. However, if such actions are implemented, relief in hospital bills for American citizens would be substantial and appreciated by all, especially the so-called middle class.

It is argued that disclosing prices in advance would help patients select the least expensive options. From my recent experience, the price disclosed for my routine prenatal care was similar to that provided to my friend receiving services at Norton Hospital, another local hospital. I am not sure whether this is a coincidence or the result of some form of common agreement drafted by the hospitals. I was told by Baptist East Hospital that the figure was just an estimate that may or may not increase. At the time I was interested in those data, the hospital had already pulled my routine visit bills offline. I cannot tell with certainty whether it did increase or not. Since health care costs in this country are very high, I purposely delayed my routine prenatal care for five and half months, hoping for a substantial decrease in my bills. However, this strategy was of no help. I was charged as if I had started my routine visit the first pregnancy month. This is unbelievable. I've come to understand that hospitals are just there to make money. It should be stressed that the services provided are generally of good quality; however, this does not justify in any way the extremely high health care costs. European hospitals purchase a great deal of tools from US industries but provide quality service to patients at an affordable price.

Why should a couple of seconds of CT scan cost $4,659.10?

Why should six days of hospital stay cost $8,862?

Why should a couple of medications and IVs at a hospital cost $5,897.55?

Why should a couple of hours of labor/delivery cost $4,883.10?

The fees I was charged for child delivery were over $42,000. From this amount, $11,000 was attributed to services rendered to the baby. According to the American Community Survey's five-year estimates, 56.8 percent of full-time year-round workers in the United States earn $49,999 and below (Census Bureau, 2014d). How can low-income and middle-class workers pay off such bills? Funny enough, some hospitals do not even give enough time to patients to pay off their bills. After two to three months, bills are sold to collection companies unless an agreement has been reached for a payment plan. For insured patients, adjustments to bills are made, depending on the negotiation skills of the insurance company. Therefore, the final amounts charged do not always correlate with the services rendered; instead, a strategy is put into place to heighten profits as much as possible at the expense of patients. Hospitals gamble on the fate of their patients. The uninsured are doomed and loaded with thousands of dollars of needless hospital bills. Meanwhile, insurers use their negotiation powers as a tool for advertisement.

With regard to my CT scan fee, let's assume that the insurance company made no adjustment, with the whole amount required to be paid. Let's also assume that the most expensive MRI, estimated at $500,000, was used. Let's further assume an average of five CT scans were performed per day (this is an underestimation, considering the patient line in the waiting room). If all of the above suppositions are true, a hospital could easily make an estimated gross income of $8,386,380 a year on CT scans alone. This allows them to pay some CEOS over $2 million a year (Cox 2011). It is outrageous that some humans live in paradise on earth at the expense of others. As mentioned above, health care institutions justify high bills by claiming, among other things, that they help pay for patients unable to do so, in this way forcing patients to involuntarily carry other people's load. Meanwhile, fierce capitalists always claim that it is unfair to use taxpayer money for social endeavors. Nevertheless, it seems fair to pile up bills for patient A by thousands of dollars in order to cover what patient B cannot pay because such activity nurses their greed. Another outrageous aspect is that, after finding ways for the hospital to get overpaid for services by all means, patient B does not go unpunished, with his/her bills sent to collection agencies. Yes, there is no mercy in the capitalist world.

Summary

In summary, the health care problem in the United States cannot be solved unless it is tackled at it roots. Although some health care plans offer better coverage than others, it does not really matter whether we have Obamacare, Trumpcare, or Anyonecare. The real American health care problem stems mainly from its high cost. As long as the cost issue is not addressed, a solution is impossible. Capitalism at its core is as cruel as socialism. A combination of both systems should be implemented in any given society so that the philosophy of one should alter the cruel extremism of the other.

A CT scan should be less than a hundred dollars.

A hospital bed should not cost more than eighty to one hundred dollars per day.

The government should regulate costs to protect citizens, therefore rendering health care accessible to all individuals, with or without insurance. Insurance companies should actually pay bills instead of being a tool for selecting who gets care and who does not. Instead of sending patients away due to financial hardship, as stated by Schneider, health care institutions should put greed aside and lower bills. In the present situation, even with insurance, many folks still cannot easily make due payments after insurance contributions. Coupling income increase and/or involving all workers in bonus sharing with decreased health care bills would boost the well-being of

Americans mightily. Furthermore, the work environment crisis should be addressed in order to promote health and prevent chronic diseases. As it is commonly said, prevention is better than cure.

Acknowledgments

Special thanks to God, who inspired me to write this book. I never thought of myself as a writer. I am still in awe of this miracle from God. I am so grateful. Glory to God! I extend my gratitude to my husband, Calvin Kouokam, for his outstanding editing work, as well as to my brother Sidoine Paulin Tuete and friend Hugues Souop for critical review. I am also indebted to Emma Engelson, who provided updated information about the Swedish social system. Finally, I acknowledge our beloved children, Anne Marie, Joash Daniel, Ruth Promise, Christiane Mercy, and Lydia Victory.

About the Author

Author Ernestine D. Motouom was inspired to write her new book by her own harrowing journey through the world of business and wage slavery. The result, *Modern Slavery: The Story of My American Dream,* makes the most of her unique perspective as both insider and outsider—she is an insider who must deal firsthand with these aspects of American society, and she is an outsider, originally from Cameroon, who lived in Germany and Sweden before immigrating to America.

Motouom provides a fresh and much-needed look at some of the most systemic ills facing US society. What's more, she also offers some possible solutions based on the approaches she saw taken in Germany and Sweden, discussing them in a matter-of-fact way rarely seen in American writing on these topics.

A married mother of five, Motouom has her master's degree in marketing and public health. She and her family live in Louisville, Kentucky.

References

American Pregnancy Association. 2013. Retrieved from http://americanpregnancy.org/unplannedpregnancy/ abortionemotionaleffects.html.

Census Bureau. 2014a. "Employment Status." 2010–2014 American Community Survey 5-Year Estimates. http://factfinder.census.gov/faces/tableservices/ jsf/pages/productview.xhtml?pid=ACS_14_5YR_ S2301&prodType=table.

Census Bureau. 2014b. "Poverty Status in the Past 12 Months." 2010–2014 American Community Survey 5-Year Estimates. http://factfinder.census. gov/faces/tableservices/jsf/pages/productview. xhtml?pid=ACS_14_5YR_S1701&prodType=table.

Census Bureau. 2014c. "Poverty Status in the Past 12 Months of Families." 2010–2014 American Community Survey 5-Year Estimates. http://factfinder.census. gov/faces/tableservices/jsf/pages/productview. xhtml?pid=ACS_14_5YR_S1702&prodType=table.

Census Bureau. 2014d. "Earnings in the Past Twelve Months." 2010-2014 American Community Survey Estimates. Retrieved from https://factfinder.cen-sus.gov/faces/tableservices/jsf/pages/productview. xhtml?pid=ACS_17_5YR_S2001&prodType=table.

Consumer Protection Financial Bureau. 2017. "Consumer Experiences with Debt Collection." www.consumer-finance.gov.

Cox, J. 2011. "First Coast Hospital CEOs Pay a Complex Formula." http://jacksonville.com/news/health-and-fitness/2011-05-31/story/first-coast-hospital-ceos-pay-complex-formula.

Federal Trade Commisssion. 2013. "The Structure and Practices of the Debt Buying Industry." https://www.ftc.gov/sites/default/files/documents/reports/structure-and-practices-debt-buying-industry/debtbuyingreport.pdf.

Golberg, J., 2014. "The Effect of Stress on Your Body." WebMD. http://www.webmd.com/balance/stress-management/effects-of-stress-on-your-body.

Gunja, N., and J. A. Brown. 2012. "Energy Drinks: Health Risk and Toxicity." *Medical Journal of Australia* 196, no. 1: 46–49.

Guttmacher Institute. 2013. "Abortion Statistics: United States Data and Trends." http://www.nrlc.org/Factsheets/FS03_AbortionInTheUS.pdf.

Guttmacher Institute. 2016. "Abortion Patients More Likely to Be Poor in 2014 Than in 2008."

https://www.guttmacher.org/news-release/2016/abortion-patients-more-likely-be-poor-2014-2008.

Hanford, E. 2016. "The Case against For-Profit Colleges and Universities." http://americanradioworks.publicradio.org/features/tomorrows-college/phoenix/case-against-for-profit-schools.

Lauer, R. H., and J. C. Lauer. 2011. *Social Problem and the Quality of Life*. 12th edition. New York, NY: McGraw-Hill Companies, Inc.

Munro, D. 2014. "Med Students Give Sober Assessment of Future with 500K in Student Debt." https://www.forbes.com/sites/danmunro/2014/01/30/med-student-gives-sober-assessment-of-future-with-500k-in-student-debt/#237e0d7d5b30.

Reinhardt, U. E. 2009. "Reimporting American Drugs from Canada." *The New York Times*. https://economix.blogs.nytimes.com/2009/12/18/reimporting-american-drugs-from-canada/.

Schneider, M. J. 2011. *Introduction to Public Health*. Third edition. Sulbury, MA: Jones and Bartlett Publishers.

Schulte, F. 2012. "Hospital 'Facility Fees' Boosting Medical Bills, and Not Just for Hospital Care." Retrieved from https://publicintegrity.org/health/hospital-facility-fees-boosting-medical-bills-and-not-just-for-hospital-care/.

Social Security Administration. 2016. "Wage Statistics for 2014." https://www.ssa.gov/cgi-bin/netcomp.cgi?year=2014.

Torres, A., and J. D. Forrest. 1988. "Why Do Women Have Abortions?" *Family Planning Perspectives* 20, no. 4:169–176.

US Bureau of Labor Statistics. 2014. "Consumer Expenditure: 2014." http://www.bls.gov/news.release/cesan.nr0.htm.

Wanjek C. 2015. "Energy Drinks Raise Blood Pressure, Study Finds." http://www.livescience.com/50178-energy-drinks-blood-pressure.html.

Zeratsky, K. 2015. "Can Energy Drinks Really Boost a Person's Energy?" http://www.mayoclinic.org/healthy-lifestyle/nutrition-and-healthy-eating/expert-answers/energy-drinks/faq-20058349.

www.ingramcontent.com/pod-product-compliance
Lightning Source LLC
Chambersburg PA
CBHW071337290326
41933CB00039B/1294